*modern wedding etiquette

essentials

carolyn humphries

foulsham
LONDON • NEW YORK • TORONTO • SYDNEY

foulsham

The Publishing House, Bennetts Close,
Cippenham, Slough, Berks, SL1 5AP, England

ISBN 0-572-03004-5

Cover photograph © Powerstock

A CIP record for this book is available from the British Library

Printed in Great Britain by Cox & Wyman Ltd, Reading

Contents

Introduction

Congratulations, there's to be a wedding! It's supposed to be the happiest time of your life, but whether you're the bride-to-be, the groom or one of the parents or guardians, the run-up can be pretty stressful. There is a lot of planning, formality and etiquette to get just right. This book is designed to give you all the information you need. It is based on personal experience and anecdotal evidence of what should and should not be done!

If you saw the film *Four Weddings and a Funeral*, you'll know that most brides don't want to look like a giant meringue. You'll also know that the ceremony should be moving, not mortifying, and the rings need to be produced on time. And when it comes to the reception, no one really wants to suffer the horrors of a best man's speech about lewd past conquests or old Aunt Gertrude getting drunk and disorderly!

With the help of this book, you can find out exactly what there is to do, when it should be done and by whom. You can create a well-oiled machine (and no, I don't mean that in an inebriated sense) that will make the whole day run smoothly and seamlessly. Not only the wedding party but all the guests will be much happier if they are gently guided through the whole occasion, knowing where they're supposed to stand or sit, where they're supposed to go and when.

As well as advice on all of that, I've included lots of customs and superstitions, many of which date back to the days when people feared evil spirits and turned to magic charms to make their good luck. It appears that weddings were a time when the malevolent spirits would do everything in their power to spoil the day and the newlyweds' future happiness. Charms and rituals were the only way to keep the bride and groom safe and many of these survive to this day. You will find these throughout the book – just look for the 🔔 icon.

On a more practical level, there are also lots of hints and pieces of useful information – marked ☺ – to help with your planning and preparation and, last but not least, plenty of cost-cutting tips, marked ✂£.

By the time you buy this book, you're probably already engaged, so let's get straight down to the nitty-gritty of organising the wedding.

Chapter 1
The Formalities

Getting married is not just a personal commitment, it's a legal one, so there are quite a few formalities to recognise. Check these out before you start so that you are clear about any licences or documents you need, and restrictions or rules you should consider in your planning.

Marriage and the law

Before you actually tie the knot, you must be sure it is legal for you to do so!

Are you old enough?

- Throughout the UK you can legally marry at 16. In Scotland you don't need the consent of your parents. In England, Wales, Northern Ireland and Guernsey, unless you've been married before, you need written parental consent if you are under 18. In Jersey, your parents must agree to the marriage if you are under 20 years old.
- If there are no parents or guardians to give consent or you feel it is withheld unreasonably or unjustly, you can apply to your local magistrates court for a decision.

Are you free?

- Both parties must be free to marry. You cannot marry if you are already married. If either party is divorced, a decree absolute must be produced.
- Both parties must be capable of understanding what they are doing and it must be of their own free will.

Who can you marry?

- The marriage must be between members of the opposite sex (by birth).
- You cannot marry members of your immediate family (grandfather, grandmother, father, mother, brother, sister, uncle, aunt, nephew, niece). You can marry a first cousin, but it's best to get medical checks first, as there is a higher risk of any abnormalities in the family being passed on to any children you may have.
- You cannot marry an adoptive parent, son or daughter.
- You can marry a step-relative provided that you are both over 21 and that the younger party was not brought up, whilst under the age of 18, in the same household as the older party.
- In England, Wales and Scotland (but not Northern Ireland) brothers- and sisters-in-law can marry. But you can only marry a parent-in-law providing you are both over 21 and both the other people involved in creating the in-law status in the first place are dead. So, for instance, a woman could marry her father-in-law only if both her husband and his

mother (her mother-in-law) are dead. Other restrictions may apply in some religious denominations.

When and where can you marry?
- At present, the marriage must take place between 8 am and 6 pm (this does not apply to Jewish or Quaker weddings).
- Weddings cannot take place on Good Friday or Christmas Day. They are not usually allowed in churches on Sundays or in a synagogue on the Sabbath.
- A wedding must not be in private, behind locked doors. This is why the doors are always left open during the ceremony.

What documents do you need?
- All weddings except Church of England ceremonies require a licence, which has to be applied for in advance (see page 16).
- All relevant documents must be handed to the officiating minister or registrar prior to the ceremony or it cannot go ahead.

For more information about relatives and who you can or cannot marry, contact the superintendent registrar for your area (the address and telephone number will be in the telephone directory under Registration of Births, Deaths & Marriages) or from the Family Record Centre (see page 185).

Who can perform the ceremony?

Your marriage must be solemnised by an authorised person who can be any of the following:

- Superintendent registrar
- Registrar
- Ordained minister of the Church of England
- Authorised minister of another religion. But, if the marriage is to be in a place of worship other than the Church of England, you must obtain a licence from your local register office.

Later in this chapter, you will find full information on the different types of wedding and how to arrange them.

The type of wedding for you

There are four types of wedding you could choose: a religious ceremony; a civil ceremony in a register office; a civil ceremony at an approved venue; or a wedding overseas, such as on a tropical island or in a Las Vegas chapel.

The civil ceremonies have the option of a blessing in church at a later date, if required (see page 156 for further details). The legal proceedings of a civil marriage are the same whether in a register office or another registered venue.

The religious ceremonies referred to in detail in this book are Christian ones; for other religions I would suggest that you refer to specific publications and seek advice from your religious leaders.

> ➤ **Same-sex weddings**
>
> At present, the British Government has no plans to allow same-sex couples to marry but it is proposing a new legal status of Civil Partnership. The new plan would include England, Wales and Scotland, but there is no decision yet on Northern Ireland. Some other countries already have legislation in place.
>
> At the time of going to press, gay or lesbian couples in the UK can only have a ceremony to celebrate their love and commitment to each other. Some boroughs will register the union but, in law, both parties will still be recognised as single people. However, there are then ways of making sure the future is secure legally: a joint mortgage; a will naming the other partner as inheritor; life assurance policies with the partner as beneficiary and so on. Visit www.pinkweddings.biz for more information on organising a celebration and securing the future.

There are different legalities according to where you live in the UK and they are all listed in the next few pages. Read the sections relevant to you carefully – they may help you decide which type of wedding you want to choose.

Documentation

Whether you are planning a religious or civil ceremony, when you apply to get married you will have to produce official documents. In general, these are:

- Birth certificates or passports
- If previously married: the death certificate of the former spouse; relevant divorce papers (remember in England and Wales you must have the decree absolute – the decree nisi does not allow you to remarry); or marriage annulment or dissolution papers
- If marrying someone from abroad: their passport or other accepted identity document and proof that the marriage will be legal according to the laws of their country

Make sure you have all of these to hand when you submit your application. Note that you should produce originals. Copies and photocopies are not normally accepted unless officially certified as a true copy by the issuing authority.

Getting married in England and Wales

The marriage can take place in three ways:

- According to the rites of the Church of England
- According to the rites of another religious denomination
- By civil ceremony

The following sections will give you all the details you need for each of these. Contact addresses for organisations that can provide further information are on pages 186–8.

Church of England marriages

The following is the law as it stands at the moment. However, in July 2002 the General Synod agreed that a major shake-up was needed in the Church of England, so it may soon be possible for you to have a religious service in all sorts of venues – much like a civil ceremony. At the time of going to press, no timescale for these changes has been decided.

It is usually expected that both of you will have been baptised (even if you are no longer regular church-goers). The marriage is solemnised by a minister of the church. If you have a family member or friend who is a minister authorised to perform weddings, you may invite him or her to officiate. It is usual for your parish minister to also be present and to have some part in the ceremony.

The marriage can take place in any church or chapel of the Church of England or Church of Wales, or an Armed Forces Chapel. Everything can be organised with the minister and there is no need to contact the registrar.

The formalities

Usually one of you needs to be living in the parish where you wish to be married. But if, for instance, it is the bride-to-be's family parish and her parents are still resident there, this is not necessary.

Banns
- These are a public announcement to the parishioners of the church where you plan to be married. It is when everyone is asked if they know any reason why you can't be legally wed.
- The banns will be called on three separate Sundays before the wedding.
- If you both live in the parish where you plan to get married, your minister will publish the banns in this church only. But if, for instance, it is only the bride's parish, banns have to be read in the groom's parish too. A certificate (valid for three months) is issued from the church not being used and must be forwarded to the minister at the designated church.
- If neither of you lives in the parish where you want to get married, one or both of you will have to live there for a period before the ceremony can be performed. Or, instead of banns, you will have to be married by common licence (see next page). You will have to discuss this with the minister.
- It is usual for the couple to attend at least one of the services when the banns are called (in each church, if necessary).
- The marriage must take place within three months of the banns being published (but it is usually planned the other way round – the date is set, then the banns are called accordingly).
- Two witnesses over 18 must be present at the wedding.

Common licence
- This is also known as an ordinary licence. It is a much quicker procedure and is used when, for one reason or another, you are unable, don't want or don't have time for banns to be read.
- One or both parties must live in the area the church serves for at least 15 days prior to the application.
- Only one day's notice is needed for the licence to be issued.
- Some ministers can issue a common licence; otherwise, he or she will be able to tell you to whom and where you apply in the diocese.
- One or other of you must apply in person, as you have to sign that there is no legal reason why you can't be married and that you have lived there for the statutory time.

Special licence
- This can be issued only on the authority of the Archbishop of Canterbury.
- It is granted when there is an urgent reason to marry, so normal formalities cannot be adhered to.
- Once granted, the special licence is valid for three months and any vicar in any place may perform the ceremony, regardless of where the parties live, providing two witnesses over 18 are present.

For a special licence contact the Register of the Court of Faculties (see page 186).

Superintendent registrar's certificate

This is not often used, but you may get married in church with a Superintendent registrar's certificate (see Civil ceremonies, page 19) but only if your minister agrees.

Other denominations and faiths

For all denominations other than the Church of England or Wales, you will have to give notice to the superintendent registrar (see Civil ceremonies, page 19) as well as contacting your religious leader (see individual entries below).

Roman Catholic marriages

The laws are similar to an Anglican wedding, but you will have to give at least six months' notice – preferably longer – of your intention to marry. This is to allow time for essential preparation according to the faith. Banns will be read, as in Church of England marriages. If only one of you is Catholic, there is a different format and banns will not be read. Consult your priest for further information or you can contact an organisation called Marriage Care (see page 186).

Nonconformist Church marriages

These include all the other protestant faiths, like Baptist, Methodist, Evangelical and United Reformed churches.

● The laws are similar to those of the Church of England.

● The chapel or place of worship must be registered for marriages.

- The marriage is either registered by the minister, if he or she is authorised to do so, or the local superintendent registrar.

For further information talk to your minister or contact the central office of your church (see pages 185–6).

Quaker marriages

A Quaker wedding needs to be registered by the area superintendent registrar (see Civil ceremonies, page 19), who will need to be present at the ceremony.

If only one of the couple is a Quaker, the other must be prepared to state that they will accept the wedding and will need to produce two letters of recommendation from other Quakers.

There will be the civil law marriage certificate, signed by the registrar and two adult witnesses, and one issued by the Quakers, which is signed by all present.

For further information contact the central office of the Religious Society of Friends (see page 186).

Jewish marriages

A Jewish wedding may take place anywhere – it doesn't have to be in a synagogue – and at any time except the Sabbath or any festival or fast days.

As for a civil ceremony, you'll need to notify the local superintendent registrar.

For further information contact the Jewish Marriage Council (see page 185).

Buddhist, Sikh, Muslim and Hindu marriages

The wedding must take place between 8 am and 6 pm.

Check with your religious leader if he is registered to perform marriages. If not, notice will have to be given to the superintendent registrar, who will have to be present at the wedding.

For further information visit www.church-weddings.co.uk.

➤ **Second marriages**

In England and Wales you may marry as many times as you wish in a register office, provided you are divorced and have a decree absolute, or your previous spouse is deceased. However, some ministers may refuse to marry you in church a second or subsequent time if you have been divorced but others will be sympathetic. You will have to discuss it with them.

Other denominations and religions have differing views. The Church of Scotland, for instance, will marry you if either of you has been divorced, provided you give six weeks' notice. In Scotland, too, you can remarry as soon as your divorce comes through (there is not a two-part system like in England and Wales).

The Roman Catholic Church doesn't recognise civil divorce. You must have your previous marriage annulled if you want to remarry in a Catholic church.

Civil ceremonies

If you are not having a religious ceremony, you can get married under civil law in a register office or at another venue, licensed to hold weddings. First you have to contact your local superintendent registrar in person to apply for a notice of marriage (you'll find the number and address under Registration of Births, Deaths and Marriages in the telephone directory). For all civil marriages, two witnesses over 18 must be present at the ceremony. The old system of a choice of superintendent registrar's certificate with or without licence has been replaced by a common 15-day-notice procedure and a superintendent registrar's certificate will be issued.

- Both of you must have lived in a registration district of England or Wales for seven days prior to applying for the notice.
- If you both live in the same district, both of you must go to the superintendent registrar at your local register office to give notice of your intent to marry. No one can go on your behalf.
- If you live in separate districts, you must each go in person to your local register office to apply.
- You may marry at any register office or approved venue in England and Wales but if different from where either of you lives, you will need to contact both superintendent registrars.

The notice of marriage
- The notice of marriage will state your names, ages, addresses, marital status, nationalities, occupations and intended marriage venue.
- After the notice is registered, it will be made public for 15 clear days (to allow for anyone to object!), so you must wait 16 days before getting married.
- When a notice of marriage is registered, it is valid for 12 months. If you are making plans well in advance (perhaps because of ensuring a specific venue for the ceremony and/or reception), you may be able to make a provisional booking in advance with the registrar of the district where you wish to marry. Contact your register office for more details.

For further information, contact the General Register Office for England and Wales (see page 187).

Registrar general's licence
This is used only in cases of serious illness, where the person is not expected to recover and it is impossible for them to travel to a register office or other registered venue to get married.

The healthy party must make the application to the superintendent registrar in person.

No residency qualifications apply.

The licence can be issued as soon as the notice is formally registered and allows the marriage to take place anywhere, any time.

The licence is valid for three months from the time of registration.

> ➤ **Gretna Green**
>
> By tradition, in the old days a couple could become man and wife just by declaring it before an official and two witnesses. An Act of Parliament in 1745 made this illegal in England, which is why couples eloped to Scotland to get married. Gretna Green became the favourite spot because it was the first stagecoach changing post over the border in Scotland.
>
> Today it's big business. It's still a romantic idea, the setting is delightful and you can have the full works: tying the knot over the anvil, with a piper, a lucky chimney sweep – the lot. But whether you want the full religious ceremony or a simple civil one with just two witnesses and no fuss, you need to allow at least 15 days after you've filled in the marriage notice form and paid the fee – so it's not going to happen overnight. Complete packages are available. Visit www.gretnaweddings.com or telephone 01461 337971 for more details.

Marriages in Scotland

The formalities are much the same whether you are marrying in church or in a register office.

- You must get a marriage notice from a Registrar of Births, Marriages and Deaths. You can get the form from any registrar but it must be returned to the one in the area where you wish to get married.
- The notice must be submitted at least 15 days prior to the wedding but preferably at least a month in advance.
- If one or other of the couple has been married before, the minimum timescale is six weeks.
- You will both have to sign a declaration that you are legally able to marry each other (see page 8). When you return the form you will have to produce your birth certificates.
- If you've been married before, you will have to produce either a death certificate or the final divorce decree.
- The registrar will prepare a schedule, which, for a civil ceremony, will be kept at the register office. If you are having a religious ceremony, you must collect the schedule at least a week before the wedding.
- After the wedding you will both sign the schedule, along with the registrar or minister and two witnesses.
- The schedule must be returned to the registrar within three days so the marriage can be formally registered.
- If one of you lives in England or Wales and one either lives in Scotland or has parents who live there, and you wish to be

married in Scotland, you must also give notice to the superintendent registrar in your area in England or Wales (look under Registration of Births, Deaths and Marriages in the telephone directory). If, however, you wish to marry in England or Wales, you will both have to live south of the Border for a period of time before you can get married (see page 12).

For further information about marrying in Scotland, contact the General Registrar Office in Edinburgh (see page 188).

Marriages in Northern Ireland

In all instances in Northern Ireland, two witnesses over 16 must be present at the ceremony.

Religious ceremonies
Church of Ireland marriages

The laws are similar to the Church of England. You must carry out one of the following formalities.

1. Publish the banns in your parish church (see page 14). If one of you lives in England, Wales or Scotland, banns will have to be read in the local parish church there too.

2. Apply for a licence from a licensing minister of the Church of Ireland. This is similar to the common licence in England and Wales (see page 15).

3. Apply for a superintendent registrar's certificate. You can obtain the form from the register office in the district in which

one or both of you has lived for at least 14 days prior to your application (see Registration of Births, Marriages and Deaths in the telephone directory). If one of you lives in England or Wales, you will have to apply to your local superintendent registrar there too. Note that there is a seven-day lapse after the certificate is issued before it becomes valid in Northern Ireland.

In certain, urgent circumstances, you may obtain a special licence from a bishop in the Church of Ireland. You will need to ask your local minister how to apply.

Roman Catholic Church marriages

There are two ways you can marry in the Roman Catholic faith in Northern Ireland.

1. Apply for a licence from a bishop-appointed licenser. Ask your parish priest for details.
2. By superintendent registrar's certificate. You can obtain the form from the register office in the district in which both of you have lived for at least seven days prior to the application (look up Registration of Births, Marriages and Deaths in the telephone directory). If you live in separate districts, you will have to give notice to registrars in both districts.

Presbyterian Church marriages in Northern Ireland

There are two ways you can marry in the Presbyterian faith:

1. After the publication of banns, if both of you are Presbyterian.

2. If one (or both) of you has been a member of a church for at
   least one month, you must give notice to the minister of your
   intent to marry and he will issue a certificate of notice. This
   is given to a licensing minister of the presbytery and a licence
   will be issued seven days later.

For further information contact the General Register Office for
Northern Ireland (see page 187).

Civil ceremonies in Northern Ireland

A civil marriage is legal in Northern Ireland but couples are
more restricted as to where they can be married.

You must apply for a superintendent registrar's certificate
from your local register office (look under Registration of
Births, Deaths and Marriages in the telephone directory).

You will normally marry in the register office in the area
where one or both of you resides. It is possible to apply for
another venue to be used, under the Marriage (Northern
Ireland) Order 2003, but it may not be that easy!

If one party lives in England or Wales, you will have to
apply to the superintendent registrar of the local area there
too. Note that there will be a seven-day lapse between the
issuing of a certificate and it becoming valid in Northern
Ireland.

If one party is living in Scotland, residence will have to be
established in Northern Ireland prior to applying to get
married.

Marrying abroad

If you live in Britain, but plan to marry abroad, check with the consul of the country you intend to marry in for what documentation you will need to make it legal.

A marriage solemnised in accordance with the local laws of a foreign country cannot be registered in the UK. You may, however, deposit the original marriage documents at the General Register Office (in case you will need extra official copies at a later date). Only the British citizen may do this.

For further details, contact the the Foreign and Commonwealth Office (see page 187).

If you are marrying abroad but British legalities have been followed, it is likely that the marriage will be considered legal in the UK. However, in some situations a court decision may be necessary.

Marrying a foreign national

If marrying a foreign national in Britain, check with their consul what documentation is necessary. Note that a British wedding may not be accepted as legally binding in their own country, so do check first!

In general you will need to produce birth certificates, proof of identity, proof of residency, criminal records searches and a certificate proving there is no reason why you shouldn't be legally married (you can apply for this from the local register office).

If marrying at an exotic location, don't take a travel agent's word about legalities: always check with the British consulate of the country in advance to make sure.

The cost of making it legal
England and Wales

For information about fees under church law, you must contact your own minister as they vary.

The civil fees for your notice of marriage from the registrar and also for the registrar's attendance at a religious ceremony or at the register office are set nationally. However, if you are marrying at a different approved venue (like a hotel), the local authority sets the fee for the registrar on the day.

Superintendent registrar's certificate (whether both in one district or in separate districts) for civil or religious ceremony	£60.00
Fee for registrar at register office wedding day	£34.00
Fee for registrar at a place of worship on the day (unless the religious leader can register the marriage)	£40.00
Fee for registrar at another licensed venue on the day varies according to local authority, the day and time	£100–£300 (approx)
Fee for a copy of the marriage certificate (per copy)	£3.50

Other fees may be payable to:
- A religious leader or 'authorised person' officiating at a ceremony
- The owners of an approved venue other than a register office or church

Scotland

Notice of marriage (civil or religious), per person	£20.00
Fee for registrar on the day (unless a minister of the church registers the marriage)	£45.00
Fee for a copy of the marriage certificate (per copy)	£8.50
Fee for registrar at another approved venue on the day varies according to local authority, the day and time	£100–£300 (approx)

Northern Ireland

Notice of marriage (per person)	£15.00
Solemnisation of civil marriage in register office	
Monday to Friday 9.00 am to 5.00 pm	£20.00
Monday to Friday 5.00 pm to 8.00 pm	£93.00
Saturday 9.00 am to 5.00 pm	£93.00
Sundays, Bank Holidays and all other times (except those mentioned above)	£106.00

Note: There may be extra fees for a larger marriage room.

Copy of marriage registration (at time of registration)	£5.00
Certified copy of marriage registration (later)	£10.00

> ➤ **In the Navy**
> If one of the couple is a serving member of the Royal Navy, and they are planning a Church of England wedding, the chaplain or commanding officer on board ship may publish the banns. If the couple are having a civil marriage, the commanding officer can record the notice and issue the marriage certificate 21 days later. However, it is no longer legal for captains of ships to solemnise marriages.

Changing your name

It is not a legal requirement for a woman to change her surname to that of her husband when they get married. But many wish to do so and it simplifies things on legal and financial documents and even in the telephone directory!

If you are going abroad for a honeymoon and want to change your name on your passport, you should apply for this well in advance. You will need to obtain the relevant application form for a post-dated passport from a general post office and have it signed by the minister or superintendent registrar who is to marry you. However, it is not necessary to do this even if you are travelling immediately after your wedding. You simply carry your marriage certificate with you as proof of your new identity.

For more information, see The Honeymoon and Beyond, page 178.

☺ **Don't tempt fate!**
A bride-to-be shouldn't practise signing her new name before she has tied the knot – it's thought to be tempting fate for the marriage not to last.

Chapter 2
The Time and the Place

So you've checked that it's legal for you to marry and, hopefully, you've decided what type of ceremony you want. Now it's is time to get down to the serious planning.

Bear in mind that the best places for both ceremonies and receptions tend to get booked up well in advance. If you are doing things in double-quick time, you may have to be prepared to make lots of compromises. It is possible to organise a wedding in a month (I know someone who did it) but in that case you have to take more or less whatever you can get! Summer is the most popular time of year and Saturday is the most popular day – both for obvious reasons. So if you choose a different season and day, you might save yourself a few headaches.

If you are planning a honeymoon as well, you should bear that in mind, too, when picking your date. You don't want to end up in the Caribbean during the hurricane season, or in Paris in August when everything is shut.

🔔 Choosing your month

If you're unsure about which month to choose, you could be guided by the following rhyme!

Married when the year is new, he'll be loving, kind and true.
When February birds do mate, you wed nor dread your fate.
If you wed when March winds blow, joy and sorrow both you'll know.
Marry in April when you can, joy for maiden and for man.
Marry in the month of May and you will surely rue the day.
Marry when June roses grow, over land and sea you'll go.
Those who in July do wed must labour for their daily bread.
Whoever wed in August be, many a change is sure to see.
Marry in September's shrine, your living will be rich and fine.
If in October you do marry, love will come but riches tarry.
If you wed in bleak November, only joys will come, remember.
When December snows fall fast, marry and true love will last.

Apparently Queen Victoria forbade her children from marrying in May. She considered that, taking heed from the Romans who held the Feast of the Dead and the Festival of the Goddess of Chastity during that month, this was an unsuitable time.

It is very popular to marry at Easter time – especially in a Christian church – because it is not considered appropriate to marry during Lent (a time for abstinence and self-denial).

June is considered a good month because it's named after Juno, the Roman goddess of love and marriage.

🔔 **Lucky days**

Days and months have different significances according to superstition – and, sometimes, tradition. Saturday is the most popular day for weddings nowadays (except for Jewish weddings) but it wasn't always thought to be such a good idea!

Monday for wealth
Tuesday for health
Wednesday the best day of all
Thursday for losses
Friday for crosses
Saturday for no luck at all

Just to put your minds at rest, though, I married on a Saturday over 27 years ago and I reckon we've been very lucky indeed!

The time of day you get married could be important. It helps to decide first what sort of reception you want. Then work back from that, bearing in mind that, in most cases, at present the law requires you to be married between 8 am and 6 pm. For instance, if you don't want to have a wedding breakfast (the fancy term for the formal reception even if it's the middle of the afternoon) *and* an evening reception, you could get married late in the afternoon and just have an evening do. Alternatively, if you want a sit-down meal at lunchtime, then you should plan the ceremony for about 11.30 am or 12 noon at the latest. If you are happy nibbling vol-au-vents at 4.30 pm, then you could have the ceremony at about 2 pm, followed by a buffet reception.

☺ **Life on the up**

It is customary for Chinese couples to marry on the half-hour, not the hour. In this way they begin their lives on 'the up', not when the hands are moving down.

✄£ **Wedding times**
- Book early so you have the best choice of cheaper venues. You don't want to have to pay for a more expensive venue because it's all you can get.
- Get married on a weekday. Reception venues are often cheaper during the week – but do make sure your most important guests can take time off work!
- Time your wedding so that the honeymoon venue will be off-season. Definitely avoid school holidays.

Planning the ceremony

Religious ceremonies

If you are planning a religious ceremony, you must contact the minister or other religious leader first to book your chosen church or other place of worship. It should be either in the parish where you live, that is, where you are listed on the electoral roll, or one where you regularly worship.

You may marry at another place of worship, provided the appropriate legalities are followed. You may also have to contact the superintendent registrar, if your chosen celebrant cannot register the marriage.

There are plans afoot for you to be able to have a Church of England ceremony at venues other than places of worship. Ask your minister if you are interested in this.

✄£ **Church ceremonies**

To save money on your church wedding, have a simple ceremony without choir, bells or professional musicians/singers. You could also share the church ceremony with another couple.

Civil ceremonies at a register office

If you wish to marry in a register office, you can book this when you first apply for a notice of marriage. If you wish to marry in different register office from where you live, you will have to apply to that registrar as well as your own. This is not so simple in Northern Ireland (see page 25).

> **✂£ Register office ceremonies**
> This is a cheaper option than another approved venue
> (below) as the register office is inexpensive and you can
> then choose a simple reception at home or in a small local
> venue.

Civil ceremonies at an approved (licensed) venue

Not long ago you could only marry in church or in a register office. Not so now – there is a huge choice of venues that hold a special licence for marriages to take place on the premises. At the time of going to press, you cannot marry outside or in a temporary or moveable structure (such as a marquee). Many hotels and historic buildings are licensed, including lots of National Trust properties – but you might find your favourite football club or racecourse is licensed too. Most of these places provide a full wedding service so will be able to offer you complete packages, if you so wish or, at least, lots of help about what is and isn't suitable (see also Planning the ceremony, page 35). If, for instance, you wanted to marry at a rugby club, you'd have to have the ceremony indoors, but could move outside for photographs on the pitch. There are, however, plans to change the law so that you can marry anywhere, inside or out. Check with the superintendent registrar. You can obtain an updated list of all available venues from the government's Local Services

organisation (see page 189). A written copy of the list costs
£5.00. You can order it and pay by credit or debit card over the
phone or apply in writing to the address on page 189, enclosing
a cheque or postal order made payable to ONS.

Alternatively, take a look at <u>www.places-to-marry.co.uk</u>. It
lists counties and register offices, and, if you click on your
local area, it will tell you what other venues are licensed for
marriages close to you.

Planning the reception

If you are marrying in church or in a register office, you will
have to choose a separate venue for the reception. Making the
decision is often difficult since most venues will have both
advantages and disadvantages. In my opinion it's best to decide
first on the size of the party: do you want a small, intimate affair
or do you want to invite everyone you know? Next, think about
the type of refreshments: do you want a sit-down meal or a
buffet? Having sorted out these two, you should be able to
choose the most suitable venue for you.

Evening parties

It has become the norm over the last decade or so for there to be
an evening reception as well as the formal wedding breakfast.
The bride's parents are not officially responsible for this, but
many seem to foot the bill. It may be that the groom's parents
would like to pay for this or, if the bride and groom are both

well-paid mature adults, they could fund it themselves. However, as with every aspect of a wedding, it is vital that it is discussed openly at the beginning so there are no hostilities and everyone is happy with the arrangements. Whoever is paying should have the final say in the planning but, usually, the evening is more a young people's event and the bride and groom oversee it.

The evening party tends to be a disco with dancing and a buffet laid on. Sometimes older guests from the formal reception take their leave; others will stay to the very end.

☺ **Don't be greedy!**
If the bride's parents are paying for the reception, you must consider their financial circumstances – if you were paying for it yourselves you would! It's all very well having a dream of a huge, lavish reception with tables laden with exotic food, hundreds of guests and Champagne flowing but it may not be financially viable. I know a bride who, when she decided to get married recently, simply announced to her parents where she wanted the reception, what she wanted and how much it would cost. They were horrified, as the money they had put by for a wedding wouldn't nearly cover it. But they didn't want to spoil her day, so they re-mortgaged their house!

Members of the wedding party – especially the bride and groom – should make sure they are available to greet any guests arriving just for the evening. There is nothing worse than arriving at a 'do' when many people have been partying for hours, not knowing anyone and wondering what to do or where to go.

Have some drinks available to welcome the new guests as they arrive (even if there is a paying bar for the evening) and introduce them to other guests so they mingle quickly.

If there isn't going to be an evening reception laid on and the bride and groom are going to be leaving for their honeymoon anyway, the best man and the ushers could organise a bash for all their contemporaries. This will avoid that awful 'flat' feeling everyone will get if they have to go home in the late afternoon or early evening. It may be possible to have it in a room at the same venue as the wedding or a pub nearby, or, if the reception was at the bride's home (especially if it was in a marquee), make use of that. You'll need to organise it in advance – you can't just suddenly decide when the bride and groom leave that you all want to continue the party without them, regardless of what the manager of the venue may think!

When I got married, the reception was in a marquee on my parents' lawn so the best man and ushers planned a party there, with my parents' agreement. They laid on music, beer, wine and simple food – lots of bread and cheese – and the 'olds' left them to it. My new husband and I had already left for the honeymoon but I gather that everyone had a great time. All those who wanted to crashed out in the tent for the night and in the morning took it in turns to cook breakfast for the next group to get up, while my mum laid on the eggs, bacon, black coffee and paracetamol!

✂£ All-in-one
If you have the ceremony late in the day, you can have just one evening reception, which keeps the costs down.

The food

A lot depends on your budget and the number of guests. Once you've decided on numbers, you can choose whether you want a sit-down affair with waiters serving several courses, a self-service buffet or a stand-up finger buffet. This, in turn will depend on the venue, whether you're having it at home in the house, in a marquee, in a hired hall or a hotel. If you've chosen to have the reception in a special place, such as a football club, you may have to use their caterers (like in a hotel) but it may be possible to employ your own, depending on the circumstances.

Start planning well in advance, so that you can get quotes from several caterers. If you are limited to the caterer at the chosen venue, ask them for lots of sample menus.

If any of your guests have special requirements, for example, vegetarian, vegan, gluten-free or dairy-free diets, make sure your caterers know well in advance. There are more tips in the reception chapter starting on page 158.

If you are having a sit-down meal with a choice of courses, you may need to send the menu to your guests with their invitations, so decisions have to be made soon!

You will not need to notify the caterers of final numbers until the invitation replies are in – most ask for about a week to ten days' notice. At the moment you are just talking approximations.

✂£ **Up close and personal**

Have an intimate wedding breakfast with close friends and family – those people you *really* want to celebrate with. You don't have to have long-lost cousins or work colleagues you hardly know.

The drink

At this stage, you will only need to know who is providing the drinks. This may be your caterers, or the hotel or licensed premises where you are holding your reception or you may be purchasing them yourselves. It will make a difference to your budget as hotels will charge 'bar prices' for all drinks and even if you ask to provide your own wine, they will charge corkage, which may be several pounds per bottle. If you are using ouside caterers, you will be able to purchase your drinks from a retailer much more cheaply. See page 160 for further details. I am sure it goes without saying that if the premises are unlicensed (such as a marquee in your garden) you cannot ask your guests to buy their alcoholic drinks, so all the drinks must be provided free.

✂£ Drink up

If you're having a large reception, you can have it in a pub or in unlicensed premises and apply for a sale-of-alcohol licence beforehand (from your local magistrates court). You can then supply as much or as little alcoholic drink as you wish – perhaps a welcoming drink and a toast only – and let guests pay for the rest themselves.

Chapter 3

The Leading Players and their Roles

Your wedding party may consist of just the bride and groom, plus two witnesses. Or it may include both sets of parents, a best man and maid of honour, any number of ushers, bridesmaids and pageboys, old Uncle Tom Cobbly and all.

Obviously, you can't choose your parents but you can choose who else you want to play all the official roles at your wedding and it's a good idea to give this plenty of thought so that both you and they enjoy the occasion to the full.

Choosing the right person for the job

Consider what you are asking your friends or relatives to do – especially the best man, who has to make a speech. It's no good choosing your best friend if he simply cannot stand up and string two words together, or mumbles into his beard. It will be cringe-making for you, for the guests – and for him. However, if you do have a best mate that you really do have to ask and you know he's not a great public speaker, make sure he keeps the speech very short and simple and suggest he follows the hints on pages 46–7 and 173. Better still, buy him one of the many books written on the subject of being a best man (see page 190).

Ask everyone in plenty of time, so they can do their jobs properly and with confidence. For the majority of them, their main tasks take place on the big day itself (with some additional prior planning). At a religious ceremony, there are particular traditions that most people adhere to, but the same ones can also apply at a civil ceremony – and, in my opinion, it makes it more 'special' if you do have some, if not all, of them.

Here is a brief résumé of the main players and what they do on the day, so, when you ask them, you can tell them what will be expected. I stress these are *not* obligatory. For exactly who does what every step of the way, see Chapters 7 and 8.

🔔 The wedding party

Evil spirits must be thwarted on your wedding day! The wedding party was originally made up of a group of young people, all similarly dressed to the bride and groom. This was done to confuse the little demons as to who were the bridal couple and prevent them from doing any dastardly deeds. Nowadays, the wedding party are chosen to play specific roles but it is still quite common for the bride to choose a similar style of dress for her chief bridesmaid (but not identical) and the best man may well be dressed similarly to the groom.

Someone to give the bride away

This is usually the bride's father, but if he cannot take on this role, she can substitute her guardian, her nearest close male relative or a very special friend. He has several duties to perform and his is a central role, so if you are choosing, bear this in mind.

- He accompanies the bride to the ceremony.
- If it is a church ceremony, he walks her down the aisle on his left arm and 'gives her away'. If it is a civil ceremony, there is no 'giving away' but he can still escort the bride to the front of the room.
- He may be invited to be one of the two official witnesses.
- He makes the first speech at the reception (see page 172) and proposes the toast to the bride and groom.

The best man

This is usually a best friend, brother or other close relative of the groom. His duties are quite extensive and crucial to the smooth running of the whole day, so great care and tact may be required when you are choosing who fulfils this role!

🔔 **The best man ... for a fight!**
The best man dates back to Anglo-Saxon times when a bride was singled out by a man to take for his wife. He would often kidnap her from her home, with his best friend in tow to help him out if there was a fight.

- He looks after the groom before the wedding.
- He is keeper of the rings.
- He is responsible for paying the minister (not usually from his own pocket, however – see Who pays for what?, page 85).
- He may be invited to be one of the official witnesses.
- He supervises the transport from the ceremony to the reception.
- He makes a speech, including the toast to the bridesmaids.
- He reads out telemessages and cards from well-wishers.

☺ **Preparing a speech**

For most people, making a speech is a daunting task. Here are a few hints on how to approach this knotty problem.

- Think about it well in advance and jot down random thoughts as you have them.
- When you've had a good few ideas, shape them into a natural progression of ideas. You don't have to use everything that occurs to you – narrow it down to the best bits. Keep it short and sweet.
- Never say anything that could possibly offend anyone, even in fun. Remarking on the labels on the soles of the groom's new shoes, or saying the bride looked just like the cake – big, white and fruity – may not go down as well as you expected.

- Anecdotes are only amusing if they are short and relevant. A 'shaggy dog' story will just bore everyone to tears and make them squirm with embarrassment.
- Try to avoid hackneyed phrases or clichés.
- Write out your speech and try to memorise most of it.
- Write cue cards to remind you of the main points and their order. This is much better than reading the speech verbatim and it really doesn't matter if it isn't word for word what you planned as long as you remember all the vital bits.
- Speak more slowly than when talking normally.
- Try to keep your hands still – don't fiddle with your notes or things in your pockets.
- Practise delivering the speech. In front of the mirror, your mother, the dog – anyone who'll listen. The more you do it, the easier it will get.

The chief bridesmaid or matron-of-honour

This is usually a sister or girlfriend of the bride. She should be at least 12 years old, especially if there are younger bridesmaids too. If you have two adult sisters or close friends you want to ask, rather than choosing just one, simply dispense with the title and let them share the duties. The chief bridesmaid's main duties are as follows.

- She helps the bride get ready before the ceremony.

- She looks after any younger attendants, often with the help of the bride's mother.
- She holds the bride's bouquet during the ceremony.
- She may be invited to be one of the two official witnesses.

Bridesmaids

These may be female relatives or friends of the bride and groom, or daughters of friends. There can be as few or many as you wish and they may be of any age. They have only limited duties but it is as well to not to have too many very young ones – they get bored very quickly and it is surprising how much noise and disruption they can cause. Of course, for some people, that simply adds to the joy of the occasion!

🔔 **Three times a bridesmaid …**
They say, 'Three times a bridesmaid, never a bride'. I panicked on my third time, when I was the ripe old age of 12. Then, my best friend married when she was only 18, and I was duly roped in again – so in the end it was four times for me and married to boot!

- At a traditional wedding, they walk behind the pageboys and chief bridesmaid. But if they are very small, the chief bridesmaid may walk behind them, to keep an eye on them.
- If there are several, they should walk in pairs, preferably organised in height/age order, with the smallest in front.

Flower girls

These are similar to bridesmaids and are usually quite young. The same cautions apply.

- They walk in front of the bride down the aisle or walkway, throwing flower petals in her path. (Obviously, you must check in advance that this is permitted in your chosen venue.)

> ♤ **Flower girls**
>
> Flower girls date back to Roman times when a young girl scattered flower petals in the path of the bride and her attendants on the way to the ceremony. The carpet of fragrant flowers was thought to help prevent malevolent spirits from working their evil.

Pageboys

These are usually very young boys, either family members or the offspring of very close friends. One or two is usually plenty – do bear in mind that, like the bridesmaids, if you have several they are more likely to get bored and, possibly, disruptive during the service. Their duties are quite simple.

- They walk behind the bride, holding her train if there is one.
- One may be a ring-bearer, who carries the rings on a cushion, which he holds out to the best man when the minister asks for the rings.

☺ **Boys will be boys – especially little ones**

A little pageboy may look angelic but if you have one, make sure his mum is sitting by the aisle or walkway near where he is going to be standing during the ceremony so that she can take him to sit with her if necessary (this also applies to tiny bridesmaids). Make sure, too, that he knows exactly what he is going to be doing. I went to a wedding in Spain where the three-year-old page, instead of holding the train, proceeded to jump on it every few seconds all the way down a very long aisle. Guests had to keep grabbing him before he yanked it off completely!

Ushers

These usually include one man from the groom's friends or family and one from the bride's side. If it is a very big wedding, you can have more. As a rule of thumb, you will need one usher for every 50 people. Their duties involve, for the most part, supervising the movement and seating of the guests, so this is a good choice for brothers, cousins and close friends who you don't want to leave out.

- They arrive at the church or ceremony venue early and stand near the door to hand out the 'order of service' sheets.
- They show people to their seats before the wedding starts – the bride's guests are seated on the left, the groom's on the right. Obviously, if there are more people invited by the bride

than the groom (which can happen), latecomers will be invited to sit wherever there is room.

- They help the best man to make sure everyone knows how to get to the reception and has transport.
- They make sure all the guests are looked after at the reception.

Who does what, when and where

Once you've chosen your wedding party, you need to get down to the serious planning of every aspect of the wedding. The bride and her mother are likely to do the bulk of the planning and organising. It is best, however, to involve the groom and his family as much as possible (they won't want to be left out). Here, briefly, is a list of who needs to get involved with what. Later I will provide more in-depth information about particular aspects – everything from choosing the invitations to planning the ceremony.

The bride

Do try to delegate as much as possible, so you don't get overwrought. Keep copious lists, make notes of everything that still has to be done, take your time, and try to enjoy it!

After you've said 'Yes'

Once you've got over the excitement of accepting your partner's proposal, there are lots of decisions to make.

- If you aren't living together already, plan with your partner where you're going to live after the wedding.
- Decide on the budget for the wedding with your partner and both sets of parents.
- Choose your type of wedding, the venues for both the ceremony and the reception, the date and time, with your partner and both sets of parents.
- Make a guest list with your partner and both sets of parents.
- Choose your attendants. Liaise with your partner because he may have a little sister, brother or other relative you should invite to be a bridesmaid or pageboy.
- Plan the ceremony with your partner.
- Agree catering arrangements with your parents and partner.
- Order the wedding cake.
- Organise any entertainment with both sets of parents and your partner.
- Choose and buy your wedding dress and accessories. Your mother and/or chief bridesmaid will probably help here.
- Choose your attendants' outfits with your mother, the attendants and their parents, if young.
- Choose your wedding bouquet.
- Choose both rings with your partner.
- Plan the honeymoon with your partner. Make sure you have any documents you need, e.g. your passport. Plan your packing.

- Select your wedding gift list. This can be arranged with a store.
- Send out invitations and any travel and accommodation instructions, to all guests. This may be done by your mother, in which case give her the full list, with addresses.
- Keep a record of gifts as they arrive.
- Attend church with your partner for the calling of the banns, if necessary.
- Buy a gift for your partner, if liked.
- Buy gifts for attendants and parents with your partner.
- Book your hairdresser.
- Plan your hen night with the chief bridesmaid.
- Go to the ceremony rehearsal (if there is one) to confirm exactly what you have to do.

🔔 **Tears of happiness**

It is considered good luck for the bride to carry a linen handkerchief – preferably with a tinge of blue on it (for the 'something blue' theme) to wipe away the happy tears during the ceremony. It is then traditional for her to keep the hankie and pass it on to her daughter when she gets married.

On the day
- Have a leisurely breakfast and pamper yourself.
- Have your hair done.
- Get ready with the help of your mother and chief bridesmaid.
- Greet the smaller bridesmaids and pages unless you are meeting them at the ceremony venue.
- Have one small glass of Champagne (or whatever you fancy) to steady your nerves. This is not compulsory or strictly according to etiquette – but I strongly recommend it.
- Be last to set off for the ceremony, accompanied by your father, or whoever is giving you away.
- After the ceremony, be first to leave for the reception with the groom.

At the reception
- Join the receiving line with your new husband after both sets of parents. Greet all the guests.
- If it is a sit-down meal, be seated first with your new husband. Remember to start eating first (no one else can begin until you do, so don't keep them waiting!)
- Cut the cake with the groom.
- Listen attentively to the speeches and then (although in the old days frowned upon) say a few words of your own if you wish (usually just to thank everyone).
- If there is dancing, lead the first dance with the groom, then dance with your father or whoever gave you away.

- Talk to as many of the guests as possible.
- Thank everyone who has been involved.
- Get changed to go away.
- Say your farewells.
- Throw your bouquet over your shoulder before getting into the car to leave. Wave wildly as you disappear into the sunset!

🔔 **Barter with your garter**

If you don't want to throw your bouquet (some brides want to keep it to press some of the blooms as a keepsake), you could throw your garter instead (even get your husband to peel it off for you!). But, if you've been given one as 'something old', passed on to you by a married friend or relative, buy a second one and wear it as well, ready to throw to the crowd at the appropriate moment. That way you can please everybody!

After the honeymoon
- Write thank-you letters with your husband to all those who sent gifts.
- Send pieces of wedding cake to any guests who couldn't come on the day (or arrange for your mother to do this).
- Make a new will and change your name (if you wish) on all legal documents (see page 182).

The groom

Before he gets this far, it's traditional for the groom to ask the bride's father, if appropriate, for his daughter's hand in marriage. Even today, with couples often living together beforehand, most fathers still appreciate the gesture!

After the wedding is announced, most grooms like to be involved, but many feel they aren't given much say in what's about to be an enormous event in their lives. It's up to the bride and her family to involve him and his family in the planning, but the groom, too, needs to show that he's keen and willing to be actively involved from the outset.

When she's said 'Yes'

- Agree the financial side of the plans with the bride and both sets of parents.
- If appropriate, talk to your own parents about offering to contribute towards the cost of the wedding (see Who pays for what?, page 85).
- Choose the type of wedding, venues for ceremony and reception, the date and time with your partner and both sets of parents.
- Agree a guest list with your partner and both sets of parents.
- Choose your best man, and agree on ushers and bridesmaids.
- Plan the ceremony with your partner.
- Make any appropriate payments for the ceremony (see Who pays for what?, page 85).

- Plan and arrange the honeymoon with your partner. Arrange all necessary money and documentation, for example, tickets, passports and visas.
- With your partner, send out invitations and any travel and accommodation instructions to all the guests. If the bride's mother is doing them, give her a full list, with addresses.
- Choose and buy both rings with your partner.
- Buy a gift for her, if you wish.
- Buy gifts for the attendants with your partner.
- Hire or buy your suit and accessories for the day.
- Attend church with your partner to hear the calling of the banns, if necessary.
- Write a speech for the reception.
- Check with the best man to make sure you've both got everything organised.
- Arrange transport for yourself and your bride from the reception.
- Go to the rehearsal (if there is one) to confirm exactly what you have to do during the ceremony.

🔔 **Don't look back!**
The best man must make sure the groom has good luck. Once he's en route to the ceremony, he must not turn back for any reason!

On the day
- Have a leisurely breakfast, perhaps with your best man.
- Get ready in plenty of time.
- Have one small drink to calm your nerves. This isn't on the real etiquette list, but my husband assures me it's pretty essential. Beer's not a good idea, however, as you might be caught short during the ceremony!
- Arrive at the ceremony early with your best man.
- Be first to leave for the reception with your new bride.
- Join the receiving line at the reception with both sets of parents to greet the guests.
- If you're having a sit-down meal, be first to start eating with your new wife. (Take a mouthful fairly quickly, so that everyone else can start. You can then keep on talking as long as you like.)
- After the bride's father's speech, make a speech to thank your father-in-law for his good wishes and to thank your in-laws for the wedding. Also, thank everyone involved and propose the toast to the bridesmaids. Give gifts to the bridesmaids, parents and best man.
- Cut the cake with the bride.
- Have the first dance with the bride.
- When the bride's father dances with his daughter, ask her mother to dance.
- Talk to as many of the guests as possible.
- Thank everyone who's been involved.

- Get changed to go away.
- Say your farewells and drive off with your new wife.

> ☺ **Beat the jokers**
> Pack your case yourself and lock it, then hide the key.
> Someone (probably your best mate) will be determined to
> sabotage your case, filling it with confetti or some kinky
> items for your wedding night.

After the honeymoon
- Write thank-you letters with your wife to all those who sent gifts.
- Change your will.
- Make any necessary changes to legal documents. You may wish to open a bank account in your joint names, or change the mortgage to include your wife's name. Don't forget about making your new wife the beneficiary of any pension, insurances, etc., and take out any new ones as necessary.

The bride's mother
The bride's mother or guardian plays a huge role before the day, helping organise just about everything except the honeymoon and the rings! On the day, however, she has less to do. If the bride doesn't have a mother or guardian, her chief bridesmaid will fulfil this role.

After the wedding is announced

- Agree with the bride and groom what sort of ceremony and reception they want.
- Agree the budget with the bride's father, the bride and groom and the groom's parents.
- Agree who is going to pay for what (best done now so there can be no confusion later).
- Help draw up a guest list with the bride, the groom and his parents.
- Agree menus and drinks with caterers.
- Buy a wedding outfit, having first discussed the colours with the bride and then the groom's mother.
- Help the bride and groom to choose stationery.
- Send out invitations and any travel, accommodation instructions to all the guests or just those that the bride's parents have invited, if the bride and groom and the groom's parents are sending ones to their respective relatives and friends.
- Tick off the invitation replies as they come in, making a note of who can and can't come.
- If necessary, agree a seating plan for the reception with the bride.
- Order the wedding cake with the bride or liaise with a friend or relative who is making it.
- Go with the bride to choose her outfit.
- Arrange the bridesmaids' outfits with the bride and, where necessary, the bridesmaids' mothers.

- Organise the flowers and buttonholes with the bride and, if they are paying for some of them, the groom's parents.
- Arrange the transport with the bride.
- Help choose and book the photographer and videographer with the bride.
- Keep a list of who gave what present and organise the wedding present display on the day.
- Arrange accommodation, if necessary, for any members of the wedding party travelling to the area the day before the wedding (you don't have to pay for hotel accommodation though!).
- If appropriate (especially if they've travelled a long way the day before the wedding), arrange with the bride's father a formal dinner the night before the wedding for the bride, groom, adult attendants and the groom's immediate family.

On the day
- Make breakfast for the bride.
- Have your hair done.
- Make sure the best man has the buttonholes (keeping back one for the bride's father and a corsage for yourself) and order of service/ceremony sheets.
- Get ready.
- Help the bride get ready, with the chief bridesmaid.
- Travel to the ceremony with the chief bridesmaid and, perhaps, the younger attendants. If not travelling with them,

arrange in advance what time to meet them at the church or ceremony venue.

- Be the last to be seated at the ceremony before the bride arrives.
- Go with the chosen members of the wedding party to witness the signing of the register.
- Leave the church or ceremony room with the groom's father.
- Help keep everybody organised during the photographs.

At the reception
- Be first in the receiving line with the bride's father to greet the guests.
- Act as hostess for the occasion, checking that everything is running smoothly, liaising with staff as necessary.
- Talk to all the guests.
- Take charge of any gifts brought on the day (making sure they have gift tabs attached or write down immediately who they are from).
- Keep an eye on the time and give the bride a nod when and if it is time for her and the groom to go and get changed.

After the party's over
- Help pack up the presents and arrange for them to be sent to the newlyweds' home.
- Liaise with the bride and help send cake to any guests who could not come to the wedding.

- Wrap the top tier of the cake ready for the bride to store for the christening of the first baby (if that's the plan).
- Have the bride's gown dry-cleaned ready for storage.
- Organise the return of any hired outfits.
- Organise the distribution of the photograph proofs and videos for selection by the members of the wedding party and order the albums/ extra prints.

The bride's father

It's an emotional time for a bride's dad. Not only does it usually cost him a small fortune, but he has to admit, finally, that his daughter is no longer his little girl but a grown woman – and some fathers find that pretty tricky to come to terms with! However, although it is still traditional for the bride's father to pay for a lot of the wedding, in these days where couples often live together before getting married, he is not usually expected to pay for absolutely everything.

If the bride's father is not able, for whatever reason, to be involved with the wedding, this role may be taken by another male relative or friend of the family on the day.

When you've agreed to give your daughter's hand in marriage

- Get out your chequebook … No, seriously, agree the financial budget for the wedding and exactly who is paying for what so there can be no 'grey areas' (see Who pays for what?, page 85).

- Buy or hire wedding outfit and accessories.
- Pay the bills as necessary.
- Write a speech. This should include some words about the bride, as well as thanks to the guests. Propose the toast to the bride and groom.
- If appropriate, with the bride's mother, book and pay for a formal dinner for the night before the wedding for members of the wedding party who have arrived the day before the wedding (bride, groom, groom's parents and any adult attendants).
- Go to the rehearsal (if there is one) to confirm exactly what you have to do during the ceremony.

On the day
- Get ready.
- See the bridesmaids and bride's mother off in the official car to the ceremony.
- Have a small drink to steady the nerves and toast your daughter's health (don't have beer or you may feel too full during the ceremony). Have a handkerchief handy and be ready to be bowled over when you see her in her finery.
- Travel with the bride in the official car to the ceremony.
- At a church ceremony, walk down the aisle with the bride on your right arm, then take a step back and remain just behind to the left of the bride at the chancel steps until you are asked to 'give her away'. Take your seat next to the bride's mother.

Divorced parents may sit in separate pews (see page 133).

- At a civil ceremony, escort the bride to the front of the room, then step to your left to sit in the front seats.
- Join the wedding party to witness the signing of the register. Sign the register as an official witness, if asked.
- When leaving after the ceremony, escort the groom's mother.
- Leave for the reception straight after the bride and groom.

At the reception

- Be first in the receiving line with the bride's mother to greet the guests.
- Escort the bride's mother to the top table if appropriate.
- Say 'grace' before the meal unless it is being said by a minister or the best man. If non-religious, simply seat the bride and groom and then invite everyone else to sit and enjoy the meal.
- Signal the waitresses to start serving.
- Check that the wine waiters are doing their job throughout the meal.
- When the meal is over, liaise with the wine waiters to pour the Champagne or other sparkling wine for the toasts. Stand and make your speech, then propose a toast to the bride and groom.
- When the bride and groom are dancing the first dance, interrupt after a while and dance with the bride. At the same time, the groom should ask the bride's mother to dance and then all the guests join in.

- Act as host for the occasion, talking to as many guests as possible, making sure they have enough to drink, etc.
- Kiss the bride before she leaves – a dad's prerogative!

The best man

The best man's duties are many and varied, some enjoyable and some not so! He should liaise with the groom during the months beforehand, to decide well in advance exactly what needs to be done. The list below outlines his role – according to normal etiquette. As there are so many things to do, it is a good idea to involve the ushers, if there are any, in as many tasks as possible.

After being asked to do the job

- Hire or buy outfit and accessories for the wedding.
- Write a speech. This traditionally involves some stories about the groom (see page 46).
- Organise transport for you and the groom. Time the distance between where the groom will be staying the night before the wedding and the ceremony venue so he won't be late!
- Organise the stag night (see Chapter 6). The best man doesn't have to pay for it: all the men invited normally contribute. Organise safe transport home for all members of the wedding party and make sure everyone else is okay too.
- Clean the car that's taking you and the groom to the ceremony. Tie on ribbons, if appropriate.

- Meet the ushers and make sure they know what they have to do on the day.
- Go to the rehearsal (if there is one) to confirm exactly what you have to do during the ceremony.

🔔 **Lucky charm**

Traditonally, the best man should remind the groom to carry a lucky charm or mascot in his pocket on his wedding day. If the groom doesn't have his own favourite talisman, the best man asks the bride to lend a favourite handkerchief or small piece of jewellery in advance so that he can give it to the groom to put in his pocket when he dresses for the wedding.

On the day
- Collect the buttonholes, a corsage for the groom's mother and order of service or ceremony sheets from the bride's mother.
- Get ready with the groom, making sure he is well ahead of time.
- Put the rings safely in your coat pocket (unless a pageboy is acting as ring-bearer).
- Pin on own and groom's buttonholes.
- Travel with the groom to the ceremony in plenty of time.
- Give the minister order of service or ceremony sheets for the wedding party.

- Check that any musicians/singers are ready and know exactly when they are supposed to perform.
- Organise distribution of buttonholes and corsages to the ushers and the groom's father and mother.
- Stand in the front pew to the right of the groom to wait for the arrival of the bride.
- Hand over the rings when asked.
- Join the wedding party for the signing of the register. The best man may be one of the official witnesses.
- Escort the chief bridesmaid out of the church.
- Escort the bride and groom, then other members of the wedding party to their cars.
- Make sure everyone knows where they are going for the reception. Leave last.

♫ The odd couple

When the best man pays the minister, it is traditional for him to offer an extra penny or pound to make the sum an odd one. This is supposed to bring luck to the couple.

At the reception
- Join the receiving line after the groom (if you get there in time).
- If you don't join the line, circulate with guests, making sure they have a drink while the other guests are being greeted.

- Escort the chief bridesmaid to the top table if there is a sit-down meal.
- Introduce the speeches if there isn't an official toastmaster.
- Make your speech after the groom's speech.
- After the bride and groom have started the dancing, dance with the chief bridesmaid.
- Circulate and talk to as many guests as possible.

When it's all over
- Check nothing is left behind after the reception. Try to identify any belongings that have been left and return them to the owner or someone who knows them. If this is not possible, hand them to the venue manager for safe keeping.
- Pack up the presents to transport them to where they are being kept until the bride and groom return from honeymoon.
- A few days later, write a thank-you letter to the bride's parents.
- Arrange for the return of any hired outfits for yourself and the groom, if appropriate. Remind the ushers to do the same.

Chief bridesmaid

The chief bridesmaid is usually either a sister or very close friend of the bride. She can therefore offer all the support the bride may need during the planning of the wedding (which can, with the best will in the world, be quite a strain). The bride can involve her as much as she likes in the organisation of the wedding and should be there as a confidantè whenever needed.

After you've been asked to do the job

- Help choose all the attendants' outfits, and agree the finances (see Who pays for what?, page 85). Go to help the bride choose hers, if she asks.
- Help the bride make decisions about hair, make-up and accessories.
- Make sure any younger bridesmaids and pageboys know what they're supposed to do. If you don't know them already, try to spend a little time with them so they get to know you too. If they like and feel comfortable and confident with you, they are more likely to do as you say on the day!
- Organise a hen night. You don't have to pay for it all – everyone going usually contributes – but you may want to plan something special (see Chapter 6).
- Go to the rehearsal (if there is one) to confirm exactly what you have to do during the ceremony.

On the day

- Go to the bride's home to dress and help her get ready.
- Go to the ceremony with the bride's mother.
- Wait for the bride outside the church or ceremony venue.
- When the bride arrives, help arrange her veil/train.
- Walk behind the bride down the aisle or walkway.

- Take the bride's bouquet and hold it during the ceremony.
- Hand it back to her before she goes to sign the register.
- If you are an official witness, go with the wedding party to sign the register.
- Walk out of the church or ceremony room with the best man.
- Travel to the reception with the best man unless you have been asked to help supervise the younger attendants.

At the reception
- Circulate with guests, making sure they have drinks while other guests are being greeted.
- Sit at the top table with the best man if there is a sit-down meal.
- If there is a guest book, get all the guests to sign and write a few words for the bride and groom.
- When the bride and groom have started the dancing, dance with the best man.
- Help the bride change into her going-away outfit.
- Check, with the best man, that nothing has been left behind at the reception and help to get anything back to its rightful owner, if possible.

When it's all over
- Arrange for any hired outfits to be returned or have your outfit dry-cleaned.
- Write a thank-you letter to the bride's parents.

Bridesmaids and pageboys

Bridesmaids and pageboys are usually young family members (from either side), close friends or the offspring of close friends. Their main role is to look good on the day and help make the whole occasion a delight to watch as well as participate in. For younger attendants, ask their mothers to check this list.

When you've been asked to do the job
- Liaise with the bride, her mother and the chief bridesmaid about outfits. Agree the finances for the outfits (see Who pays for what?, page 85).
- Go to the rehearsal (if there is one) to confirm exactly what you have to do during the ceremony.

On the day
- Arrive at the bride's house to get ready (unless very small, when it may be more sensible for the child to get dressed at home and meet the wedding party at the venue).
- Leave before the bride and travel with the bride's mother to the church or other venue.
- Wait outside the venue for the arrival of the bride.

- Follow the bride down the aisle. Flower girls should walk in front of her, scattering the flower petals in her path. Pageboys should hold the bride's train. One may be delegated to carry the rings on a cushion.
- Remain standing behind the bride and groom during the ceremony. (If they are very young, they can go and sit with their parents.)
- Follow the bride and groom out of the church, after the chief bridesmaid and the best man.

At the reception
- If old enough, mingle with the guests.
- Younger ones can simply enjoy the party!

When it's all over
- Return any hired outfits or have outfits dry-cleaned.
- Write a thank-you note to the bride's parents (parents should do this for younger children).

Ushers
Ushers are usually brothers or close friends of the bride or groom. One usher for every 50 guests is a good idea but many couples simply have two, one from the groom's side and one from the bride's side. Their main job is to assist the best man, making sure that the guests know where to sit and what to do during the ceremony and the reception (see also The Ceremony,

page 135, and The Reception, page 177). If ushers do their job properly, the whole occasion should run smoothly, without any hiccups.

When you've been asked to do the job

- Find out the dress code and hire or buy suits and accessories accordingly. If you aren't required to wear morning dress, your own best lounge suit and a tie that's in keeping with the colours of the day (bridesmaids' dresses and flowers) will be fine.
- Beg or borrow some umbrellas to shelter guests and the wedding party if it rains.
- Liaise with the best man and help him with any tasks he may have.

On the day

- Get ready and arrive at the church or other ceremony venue early.
- Make sure you know any special seating requirements, such as for a disabled guest or for divorced parents of the bride or groom. Make sure the parents of any small bridesmaids or pageboys are sitting in a convenient position to reach their offspring if it all gets too much during the ceremony!
- Distribute the buttonholes for yourselves and the groom's father and give a corsage to the groom's mother.

- Set aside the correct number of order of service or ceremony sheets for the wedding party and either give them to the minister or put them on appropriate chairs at the front.
- Hand out the orders of service or ceremony to each guest as they arrive.
- As each guest arrives, ask whether they are a guest of the bride or groom. The groom's guests traditionally sit on the right, the bride's on the left, with the immediate family in the front and other close relatives just behind.
- Escort any ladies on their own to their seats – this includes the bride's mother, who should sit in the front left-hand seat.
- Find out in advance whether photography is allowed in the church or venue or whether confetti can be thrown in the churchyard or outside the venue, so that you can let people know accordingly.
- When the bride arrives, take your seats at the back.
- If the best man has to leave for the reception before you, make sure everyone else has transport and knows where to go.
- Check nothing has been left behind in the church or ceremony venue. If it has, collect it up and take it to the reception to find its owner.
- Drive bridesmaids and pages to the reception, if necessary.

At the reception
- Help with parking arrangements, if appropriate.
- Guide guests along the receiving line and make sure they have drinks and know where to go.
- Enjoy the party but continue to keep an eye on things, talking to as many guests as possible and providing drinks etc., if necessary.
- Decorate the going-away car with the best man.

When it's all over
- Return any hired outfits.
- Write a thank-you note to the bride's parents.

The groom's parents

It's up to individual families to decide just how little or how much input the groom's parents have in the proceedings and it is very much up to them to say early on if they would like to offer financial and/or practical help with the arrangements. If they offer nothing, they will be told how many people they can invite. The bride's mother will liaise with the groom's mother about colour schemes so their outfits don't clash. If they are involved, this is the most likely scenario.

When the wedding is announced
- Discuss and agree any financial involvement with the bride and groom and the bride's parents. It may be a general

donation to the cost or you may offer to pay for a specific part of the proceedings, say, the church flowers.

- Offer to pay for the evening reception if you wish. This may or may not be accepted.
- Draw up a guest list with the bride and groom and the bride's parents.
- Buy or hire outfits and accessories for the occasion.

On the day

- Arrive at the church or ceremony venue in good time and sit on the right-hand side, behind the groom and best man.
- Go with the invited wedding party to sign the register. The groom's father may be the one of the official witnesses signing the register.
- The groom's father escorts the bride's mother out of the church or ceremony room.
- The groom's mother leaves with the bride's father.
- Leave for the reception at the same time as the bride's parents.

At the reception

- Join the reception line after the bride's parents to greet the guests.
- Sit at the top table if there is a sit-down meal.
- Talk to as many guests as possible.

When it's all over
- Write to the bride's parents to thank them for the wedding.
- Write a thank-you letter to the bride and groom if they gave you gifts at the reception.

Who wears what?

Contrary to popular belief it isn't compulsory for the bride to be dressed in a flowing white dress and everyone else to be in their best bib and tucker. You can marry in any outfit you like (providing any points of modesty are recognised, especially if marrying in church). But, as it's the most important day in the bride's life – and that of the groom too – dressing to fit the occasion is as much a part of the proceedings as saying 'I will'. You can wear all the traditional finery, or you might like to think about having a themed wedding, especially if you're marrying in an unusual venue. For instance, you might like to get married in an ancient castle, with everyone dressed in mediaeval costume and a mediaeval banquet to round off the celebrations!

> 🔔 **Red for joy**
> In China red, not white, is the colour for weddings, signifying joy, prosperity and love and it may be used for everything from the bride's dress to the invitations.

The bride

Traditionally, a bride's white dress denotes purity and maidenhood and was first introduced for rich young brides in the sixteenth century. Later, Queen Victoria made the idea even more popular by choosing to marry in a white gown instead of silver, which royal brides had always worn before. These days, if you've already been living together for several years, it's a bit hypocritical to wear pure white, so if you want to stay with the white theme, perhaps ivory or oyster is more appropriate. Alternatively, you could go for a completely different colour.

🔔 **Colour-wise**

Married in white, you have chosen right,
Married in blue, your love will always be true,
Married in pearl, you will live in a whirl,
Married in brown, you will live in town,
Married in red, you will wish yourself dead,
Married in yellow, ashamed of your fellow,
Married in green, ashamed to be seen,
Married in pink, of you he will think,
Married in grey, you will go far away,
Married in black, you will wish yourself back.

♤ Something old, something new…

This famous rhyme dates back to Victorian times, but some of the symbolism is much older than that. The bride is supposed to wear something that represents each item in the rhyme.

Something old is traditionally a garter belonging to an older friend who is a happily married woman, in the hope her 'joy' will pass on to the new bride. It is also supposed to represent all the couple's friends in the hope they will sustain life-long friendships.

Something new is usually the dress. But if it is hired, pretty new underwear is the most popular alternative.

Something borrowed is usually a valuable (either in terms of money or sentiment) piece of jewellery, borrowed from a member of the bride's family. She must give it back after the ceremony to bring good luck and fortune.

Something blue is a symbol of fidelity. Many ancient customs depict the bride wearing blue ribbons for this reason. These days, a blue garter (or one trimmed with a blue ribbon) is popular, or underwear with blue ribbons/lace or a linen handkerchief with blue edging or embroidery.

You may have very definite ideas about what you want to wear – childhood dreams often come into play here! But, it's still a good idea – and great fun – to try on all sorts of creations before you decide. There is a huge choice of styles, not only of dresses, but of veils and head-dresses to match, and that's before you've even started looking at jewellery, shoes and other accessories. This is your big day, so make the best of it.

If you are having your dress made, allow plenty of time for fittings etc. These things don't happen overnight!

If you want something fabulous, but don't want to spend thousands, you could hire a gown. Look in your local *Yellow Pages*.

If you're on a tight budget, charity shops – Oxfam, in particular – could help. They actually have bridal boutiques in some areas and you could pay from around £10 to £500 (for a top designer creation that would normally cost you thousands of pounds in a shop).

Attendants

The chief bridesmaid may wear a different style and colour from the other attendants. It is usual for the bride to have the final say in colour and style – after consultation of course! It is also her choice for the bridesmaids and pageboys. These days it is usual for the attendants (or their parents if young) to contribute towards the cost.

☺ **Watch that waistline**

I knew one girl who always pigged out on whole packets of chocolate biscuits when she was stressed. After several contretemps with parents, fiancé, prospective in-laws and the caterers over last-minute vegetarian guests, she went for her final fitting, only to find she'd put on so much weight, the pearl buttons burst off the back of the bodice!

The opposite can happen too. Many people find they lose weight when they're stressed out. After similar scenes during the latter stages of her wedding preparations, another friend of mine tried on her outfit the week before the wedding, only to find she'd shrunk a whole dress size so her beautiful gown hung on her like a sack. Fortunately, the shop had the design in a smaller size, and a dressmaker's nightmare was averted!

The bride's mother

It is not considered good form for the bride's mother to wear white or ivory, but otherwise it's entirely up to her what colour she chooses. It's usually a good idea not to clash with the official colour scheme but she doesn't have to match it either! In the same way, the bride's mother may wish to liaise with the groom's mother to ensure their outfits complement each other. Hats and gloves aren't compulsory but it's the best excuse ever to wear them if you like them.

🔔 **More customs and superstitions**

- It's unlucky for the groom to see the bride in her wedding dress before the ceremony.
- It's thought unlucky for her to make her own dress or for her to put on the entire outfit before the day. Some brides leave one stitch on the hem to be sewn when she puts on the gown on the day. If that's too much stress, always try it on with one shoe only!
- The veil, first worn by brides in Roman times, was thought to disguise her, to ward off evil spirits.
- In modern times, the veil is thought to depict modesty and chastity – which is why the bride keeps her face covered until after the vows have been said.
- In some eastern countries, the bride's face is covered until after the ceremony and, when the veil is lifted, it's often the first time the groom has seen his wife's face!

☺ **Bigger isn't necessarily better!**

Just remember, Mums, when you're buying a hat that you are going to be sitting right at the front of the other guests. Don't wear one that's so huge it blocks everyone's view.

> ### 🔔 Who's that girl?
>
> In Roman times, bridesmaids were dressed in similar outfits to the bride, the idea being that they would confuse evil spirits, who wouldn't know which one was the real bride!
>
> Bridesmaids used to carry a drawstring Dorothy bag, now usually called a 'dolly bag' (or 'wedding purse' in the USA) containing rice, grains, sugared almonds or rose petals to throw over the bride and groom to symbolise prosperity and fertility. Today they are still frequently used, but apart from confetti they are ideal for carrying vital personal items such as a lipstick and handkerchief!

The men in the wedding party

If morning dress is going to be worn, the groom, bride's father, best man and ushers should definitely wear it and it always looks better in the photographs if the groom's father wears it too.

Traditionally the coats should be black or in a shade of grey, but green, burgundy and navy are becoming popular too. The trousers should be plain grey, if wearing a plain grey jacket, or charcoal-striped.

Waistcoats used to always be grey but now you can get some fabulously flamboyant ones, which look great if they tone with the bridesmaids' and pages' outfits. Alternatively, stick to grey but have a colourful silk tie or cravat and handkerchief to match the colour scheme for the day.

Shirts are usually white and should be hired with the rest of the outfit.

The top hat and gloves are not usually worn at the wedding; they are simply carried.

If morning dress is not being worn, then lounge suits are fine. Before deciding on ties etc., check the colour scheme with the bride if the traditional light grey isn't being worn.

Shoes are usually black, with black or grey socks.

Outfit hire
Your *Yellow Pages* will list all your local outfitters who hire wedding attire, for women as well as men. Alternatively visit www.hire-society.com or www.wedding-service.co.uk for lots of information.

Who pays for what?
In the days when girls lived at home until they got married, it was the bride's parents who footed the bill for the entire wedding. Now things have changed. Sometimes the bride and groom pay for their wedding themselves – especially if they've already set up home together and have been living as a couple for some time. In the majority of cases, although the groom's parents and the bride and groom themselves may contribute, it is true to say that the lion's share still often falls to the bride's parents.

✂£ **Fitting the bill**
- Borrow your outfits or buy second-hand (see Oxfam, page 81).
- Choose lounge suits rather than morning or evening dress (most men have a reasonable suit they can wear).
- Contact a local fashion design college and see if they want to make your wedding a 'project'.
- Get a friend or relative to make the bride's dress and bridesmaids' outfits.
- Have just one bridesmaid – or none!
- Wear individual fresh or silk flowers in your hair instead of a formal head-dress.
- Choose outfits that can be worn again.

It is vital that as soon as the marriage is announced you make a budget plan – and stick to it. A dream wedding is one thing, but one that is totally outside what you can afford will run up debts that could be impossible to pay off, and nobody wants to start married life like that. Remember that sometimes a small intimate affair, beautifully organised, may be preferable to a gigantic bash where you've had to cut corners all the way to make it financially possible at all.

Unless the bride's parents insist on paying for everything, it's best, if possible, that both sets of parents and the bride and groom should sit down together and discuss the finances. It may seem awkward at first, but it's much better if everyone has agreed and knows exactly what they are paying for. Then there can be no resentment, arguments or mix-ups later on, which could be disastrous.

Here's a list of who is traditionally responsible for which expense. I've also suggested options that may be more appropriate.

The bride's parents pay for

- The bride's wedding outfit
- The bride's going-away outfit
  The bride may pay for this herself.
- Young bridesmaids' and pageboys' outfits
  Their parents may pay, especially if the outfits can be worn again.
- The chief bridesmaid's outfit
  Her parents may pay or, if adult, she may pay for this herself.
- Official announcements in the press
- Wedding stationery, including invitations, orders of service or ceremony, cake boxes for sending cake to guests who can't attend on the day, place cards, etc.
- Flowers for the church or ceremony room and the reception
  The groom's parents may wish to pay for these.
- The reception (venue and catering)
- Photographer and videographer (this will include one set of photographs and one tape, but not additional prints for

individual guests and members of the wedding party, who should pay for their own)
- Official wedding cars
- The wedding cake
  A relative or family friend may offer to make and give this to the bride and groom as their wedding gift but they or their parents should still offer to pay for the ingredients.
- Extra decorations and finishing touches at the reception (see page 117)
  The groom's parents might like to pay as these do mount up!
- The evening party (this isn't compulsory and, technically, it isn't up to the parents to pay but they often do)
  The groom's parents could pay for this or the bride and groom may fund it themselves – unless they are not attending!

The groom pays for
- The bride's ring
- A wedding gift for the bride (optional)
- Hire or purchase of his wedding outfit
- The best man's outfit
  Nowadays the best man usually pays for this himself.
- All church, register office or other ceremony venue expenses
- The bride's and bridesmaids' bouquets and the buttonholes and corsages
  The groom's parents may like to pay for these.

- Gifts for the attendants (bridesmaids, pages, best man and ushers) and flowers for both mothers
- Some of the costs of the stag night (although all those invited usually contribute)
- Transport to take him and the best man to the ceremony and him and his bride to the reception
- Going-away transport
- The honeymoon
  If the groom's parents are not contributing in other ways, they may give a sum towards this.
- Somewhere to live when they come back from honeymoon – this cost is usually shared with his bride
  The bride's or the groom's parents may wish to give a sum towards a down payment on a mortgage as a wedding present.

The bride pays for
- The groom's ring
- A wedding gift for the groom (optional)
- Some of the costs of the hen night (although all those invited usually contribute)
- Hairdresser for herself and the bridesmaids
  The bridesmaids or their parents may pay for their hairdos.
- Personal items like make-up, jewellery, underwear, etc.

Chapter 4
The Finishing Touches

Say it with flowers

Flowers play an important part in making the occasion look perfect. Shop around several florists to get an idea of prices and styles you may like. Flowers can cost an enormous amount of money so you will have to budget carefully. Also, plan and order them well in advance. Take advice from your chosen florist about availability of different blooms and ones that are most suitable. They will be able to show you all sorts of pictures of different bouquets and displays to choose from. Once you have decided on your budget and colour scheme it is best to order the flowers at the same time from the same source so that you can be sure they match. Don't forget to include flowers – if you need them – for the car, to decorate the family home if the reception is to be there, and a bouquet each for the bride's and the groom's mother (to be given at the reception).

Flowers to be carried

The bride's bouquet is very much according to personal taste and the style of the dress. A large bouquet would complement a long, lacy dress with flowing train and veil, whereas a small posy or even a single bloom would look better with a simple, shorter dress. The bride's flowers always used to be white but now they can be any colours of the rainbow. It's usually a good idea to think of the colour scheme you want for the bridesmaids and pages first, then choose flowers that blend with this.

For the bridesmaids, small posies are most popular, picking up the colours of the bride's bouquet and those of the church or other venue. If you have little bridesmaids, tiny baskets of flowers look lovely and are easier for them to carry. But have them made of fabric or wicker, not china. At three years old I had to carry a large pottery basket of flowers down a very long aisle. It looked so pretty but was so heavy that I dropped it. Fortunately the basket didn't break but I was very upset and embarrassed! If it's a winter wedding, you could consider giving them velvet muffs with a spray of fresh flowers on them.

Head-dresses

Any fresh floral head-dresses for the bride and/or attendants should be ordered at the same time as the rest of the flowers.

Buttonholes and corsages

It's simplest to organise the buttonholes and corsages at the same time as the rest of the flowers. Traditionally buttonholes were white or red carnations, but now it's more usual to choose single flowers in a colour that match the wedding bouquets. The groom and both fathers can have double flowers if you like. It is not considered good etiquette for them to contain any foliage but, again, that is entirely up to you.

☺ **Small can be beautiful**

Large bouquets were particularly popular after the war, with long trailing greenery. They can look stunning but also can be quite cumbersome and fairly heavy – especially tricky for the chief bridesmaid when she has to hold it along with her own flowers for most of the ceremony! A small spray, beautifully arranged, can be just as effective. If you are having a religious ceremony, you could have just a small spray of orchids or other exotic flowers on a silk ribbon attached to a white or ivory prayer book. This looks particularly beautiful and demure with a long-sleeved, unfussy dress, perhaps of velvet or satin.

The corsages should be worn by the bride's and the groom's mothers, to complement their outfits. They should not be too flamboyant. Check first with the two mothers that they would like to wear them, as they are not compulsory.

Flowers for the ceremony and reception

It is usual to have the same colour scheme throughout the whole wedding.

Church

If you are marrying in church, you will have to check with the minister about a convenient time to decorate the church. You can either pay – a lot – to have it decorated professionally, or there may be a group of parishioners who usually decorate the church for Christmas, Easter, etc., who would be prepared to do it for you for a small fee or donation to the church fund. Also, check if there is to be another wedding on the same day. It may be possible to share the cost.

🔔 **What a knight!**

The groom's buttonhole should exactly match a flower in the bride's bouquet. This is based on the custom when a knight of the realm would wear his lady's colours to display his love.

Register office

The room may already be decorated with flowers, but you may be able to arrange a small display if you so wish. Check with the superintendent registrar.

Other venues

The proprietors – of the hotel, stately home or wherever – may include the flowers in their costs. Check with them and then arrange your own displays if necessary.

At the reception

You should discuss arrangements for flowers with the proprietor or manager of the venue. Many will be happy to recommend a florist that they have used themselves. Obviously, if you are having the reception at home in the house or a marquee, you will need to organise all the flowers.

✄£ **Budget ideas for flowers**

- Carry small, simple posies or a single bloom each.
- Don't have professionals to decorate the church: either arrange flowers in church yourself or buy them yourself and arrange for the parishioners who usually decorate the church to do it for you.
- Share the cost of flowers with other couples getting married on the same day.
- Have pot plants as decorations at the church and reception and take them home afterwards.
- Arrange for the flowers from the ceremony to be taken to the reception.
- Have silk flowers instead of fresh, so they can be used again.

If you are having a sit-down meal, the top table is usually decorated with flowers, but don't make any central display too big or it may block the guests' view of the bride and groom! The other tables can each have a small central arrangement or a single flower in a vase to match the bride's bouquet. Another idea is to have little pot plants as table decorations. Whichever you choose, it's a good idea to give them as gifts to chosen guests after the reception (or you could give them to a local hospice).

The meaning of the blooms

You may like to think of the symbolic meaning of different flowers and choose ones you think appropriate. Mind you, having done a lot of research, I found the meanings change from source to source. These are the ones I liked:

Flower	Colour	Meaning
Amaryllis	White/pale or dark pink	Pride
Apple blossom	White/pink	Hope
Aster	Various	Love token
Azalia	Various	Temperance
Begonia	Red/pink/yellow/white	Fanciful
Bluebell	Blue	Thankfulness
Campanula	White	Gratitude
Camellia	White	Loveliness
	Red	Excellence
Carnation	Various	Fidelity, deep love
	Pink	Motherly love
	Red	Admiration
	Striped	Unrequited love

Flower	Colour	Meaning
Carnation	White	Ardent love and devotion
Chrysanthemum	Red	Love
	White	Truth
	Yellow	Honesty
Cornflower	Blue	Delicacy
Daffodil	Yellow	Devotion
Dahlia	Various	Dignity
Daisy	Various	Innocence, gentleness
Fern	Green	Fascination
Flax (linum)	Various	Kindness
Forget-me-not	Blue	True love
Gardenia	Creamy yellow	Joy
Gladiolus	Various	Bonds of affection
Gypsophila	White/pink	Gentleness
Heather	Pink	Admiration
	White	Good luck
Honesty (lunaria)	Purple	Honesty
Honeysuckle	Cream/yellow/red	Devoted affection
Ivy	Green/varigated	Conjugal love
Jasmine	Yellow	Elegance, grace
	White	Amiability
Jonquil	Yellow	Affection shared

Flower	Colour	Meaning
Larkspur (delphinium)	Pale/deep blue	Laughter
Lavender	Blue/purple	Luck
Lilac	Purple	Unity
	White	Young love
Lily	Pink	Tolerance
	White	Purity
	Red/orange/yellow	Majesty
Lily of the valley	White	Happiness and humility
Magnolia	White/pink	Dignity
Marigold	Yellow/orange	Affection
Mimosa	Yellow	Sensibility
Orange blossom (philadelphus)	White	Purity, chastity, everlasting love
Orchid	Various	Rare beauty
Pansy	Various	Eyes only for you
Peony	White/pink/red	Bashfulness, shame
Periwinkle (vinca)	Light/dark blue	Friendship
Phlox	Various	Dreams come true
Pink (dianthus)	Pink/white	Aching heart
Polyanthus	Various	Dangerous love
Primrose	Yellow	Young love

Flower	Colour	Meaning
Rose	Orange	Desire
	Pink	Perfect happiness
	Red	Passionate love
	White	Purity
	Yellow or cream	Joy
	Various	I love you
	Red and white	Unity
Rosebud	Various	Beauty and youth
Spirea	White	Victory, conceit
Stephanotis	White	Good luck, happiness in marriage
Sweet pea	Various	Delicate pleasures
Tulip	Various	Passionate love
	Red	Undying love
Verbena	Various	Wishes granted
Violet	Violet/yellow	Modesty

🔔 Orange blossom

Orange blossom has been the traditional flower for weddings since the Crusades. The Saracens were the first to believe it symbolised chastity and purity with the green leaves symbolising everlasting love. The Crusaders brought the plant back to England and with it the custom.

Stationery

Choosing wedding stationery and having it printed is one of the earliest jobs that have to be done. As well as specialist printers, many department stores and high street stationers offer a choice of designs, both ready-printed and printed to order. You can choose invitations, place cards for a sit-down meal printed (although these can be hand-written when you work out a seating plan) and orders of service or ceremony.

The invitations

Usually the bride's parents host the wedding so the invitations are from them, inviting guests to their daughter's wedding. If, however, the bride and groom are funding the whole thing, they would do the inviting themselves.

They are usually worded in the third person – 'Mr and Mrs John Smith', or 'John and Betty Smith' or simply 'John and Betty', depending on how formal or informal the proceedings are going to be (see the sample invitations on pages 101–4).

The wording should make it clear if there is going to be an evening party as well and whether it is following on or there will be a brief interlude after the formal reception. If there is a particular dress code, this should be written in the bottom right-hand corner, e.g. 'Morning dress'; 'Black tie' (this means evening wear); 'Mediaeval theme'; 'Hats optional'.

You should also include the name and address of the person to whom the replies should be sent, and by what date (remember to allow time for giving caterers etc. final numbers).

Send the invitations out six to eight weeks before the day. Any menu choices, travel maps showing the ceremony venue and the reception venue (if different), and accommodation lists should be sent at the same time.

Do send invitations to the groom's parents, the best man and other attendants, even though they will already know all about it.

✂£ Do it yourself
- If you have a PC, you could print your own stationery.
- If you know someone with lovely handwriting or who is good at calligraphy, ask them to write the place cards.
- Buy pre-printed stationery from a stationer or newsagent.

Sample invitations

The style of the invitations should reflect the style of the wedding itself. If you are having a traditional church wedding with a proper wedding breakfast, you should send out formal invitations. These may be printed with a gap for you to fill in the names of the guests, as in the sample on page 101. If the wedding is in a register office or at a different venue, simply alter the wording to suit.

Mr and Mrs John Day
request the pleasure of the company of

....
(insert guest names here)

at the marriage of their daughter
Susan Anne
to
Mr Peter Michael Blake
at
St Andrew's Church, Whitetown
on Saturday 26 February
at 12.30 pm
and afterwards at a reception at
The Castle Hotel, Whitetown.
There will also be an evening disco and buffet
starting at 7.30 pm.

RSVP   Morning dress optional
The Beeches
1 Highbury Road
Whitetown SP1 3GY

In the next sample, you simply write the names of the guests in the top left-hand corner of the invitation. You can use more formal wording, with titles, as in the example on page 101, if you prefer.

(Insert guest names here)

John and Mary Day
request the pleasure of your company
at the marriage of their daughter
Susan
to
Peter Blake
at
St Andrew's Church, Whitetown
on Saturday 26 February
at 12.30 pm
and afterwards at a reception at
The Castle Hotel, Whitetown.
There will also be an evening disco and buffet
starting at 7.30 pm.

RSVP
The Beeches
1 Highbury Road
Whitetown
SP1 3GY

If guest numbers are very large, you may wish to invite some people to the reception only. If so, use wording as in the next example.

Mr and Mrs John Day
request the pleasure of
the company of

....
(insert guest names here)
at an evening disco and buffet
to be held at
The Castle Hotel, Whitetown
on Saturday 26 February
at 7.30 pm
to celebrate the marriage of their daughter
Susan Anne
to
Mr Peter Michael Blake

RSVP
The Beeches
1 Highbury Road
Whitetown
SP1 3GY

In some cases, the bride and groom may issue the invitations themselves, perhaps because they've been together a long time or because it is a second marriage. In this case, the wedding is likely to be a much less formal affair and the invitations should reflect this.

Susan Day and Peter Blake invite you to their wedding
at St Andrew's Church, Whitetown
on Saturday 26 February at 12.30 pm
and to a reception afterwards
at The Castle Hotel, Whitetown

RSVP
Flat 4
Watersmeet
Rivervale
TG3 8PP
Tel: 013564 477830

Replying to invitations
A reply to a formal invitation is usually made in the third person (i.e. using your name rather than saying 'I') and should be written in the centre of the paper. There is no need to add your address on the top right-hand corner of the sheet.

Mr and Mrs Jack Samuels thank Mr and Mrs John Day
for their kind invitation to their daughter's wedding
on Saturday 26 February and afterwards at the reception
and have great pleasure in accepting.

Notice of postponement of a wedding

Hopefully, this won't happen, but it could if, for instance, there is a bereavement or illness to an immediate family member. In this case, guests need to be notified and should be asked to re-confirm if they can attend. Keep it brief.

Owing to the recent death of Mrs Mary Day, the wedding
between Susan Day and Peter Blake at St Andrew's Church on
Saturday 26 February at 12.30 pm
has been postponed until Saturday 23 April at 3.30 pm.

RSVP
The Beeches
1 Highbury Road
Whitetown
SP1 3GY

Notice of cancellation of a wedding

Hopefully, this won't happen either. But if the wedding is called off, guests need to be notified. Gifts will also have to be returned. Again, keep it brief.

It is with regret that Mr and Mrs John Day
wish to inform you that the marriage between their daughter
Susan and Mr Peter Blake on Saturday 26 February
will not now take place.

The cake

If you are having a wedding cake – and not everyone does – go
to one or more reputable bakers to get quotes. You'll probably
be shocked at the prices. In their defence, the ingredients are
expensive and it takes a lot of time to hand-ice even a one-tier
cake! However, many people get a friend or relative to bake and
decorate the cake. If you're lucky enough to have that option,
go for it – it'll probably taste tons better than a bought one
anyway! You don't have to have three tiers and if you use the tip
opposite, one or two tiers will be plenty on show. You will need
to give whoever is making the cake the date and venue for the
reception, but not necessarily when you order. Check progress
with your cake-maker at least a week before the wedding, to be
sure that everything is under control.

✂£ **Cutting the cost of the cake**
- Ask someone to make the cake as a wedding present.
- Have a sponge cake – the ingredients are tons cheaper
  than fruit (but don't have pillared tiers!). For a bit of
  tradition, decorate it with sugared almonds to
  symbolise fertility.

Don't use ready-roll icing if you're making a tiered cake. The pillars will sink into the top and the whole thing will collapse!

△ **Traditions for your cake decorations**

There are traditional decorations for wedding cakes and they all have symbolic meanings. If you have other flowers on your cake see the list on pages 95–8 for their symbolism.

Bells – drive away evil spirits

Cupids – lasting love

Horseshoes – fertility and luck

Orange blossom – purity and luck

White doves – harmony in the marriage

White rosebuds – purity

Coloured rosebuds – young love

Cake-making tips

If the waiting staff at the reception have to dismantle the cake and then start cutting, it all gets a bit chaotic and takes ages! To speed things up, it's a good idea to bake an extra tier and just marzipan and plain-ice it. This can then be cut up behind the scenes, ready to be distributed to the guests as soon as the symbolic cutting of the properly decorated cake has been done, before the speeches. It also means that there will be plenty to cut and send in little gift boxes to those guests who couldn't attend on the day or those not-so-close friends or colleagues you simply couldn't invite because there wasn't room.

Cake boxes

Small boxes can be bought flat-packed, ready to make up to send tiny pieces of wedding cake to those guests who cannot attend the wedding. Buy these once you know the final number of refusals. Buy a few extras in case anyone cries off at the last moment or for any less close friend you can't invite but to whom you would like to send a token gesture.

The rings

This book is all about planning the wedding, so I'm assuming you already have an engagement ring. Just for the record, it should be worn on the woman's third finger of the left hand, to tell the world that she's already spoken for!

🔔 **With this ring …**

It's considered unlucky to buy a wedding ring at the same time as the engagement ring.

Diamonds have been the most popular stones for engagement rings since the fifteenth century. As diamond is the hardest known substance, it was thought that wearing one (or more) would ensure that the marriage would last forever.

It used to be the custom for the man to go down on bended knee to propose, producing the ring at the same time. Nowadays we are a lot more prosaic about these things, so once the proposal has been made and accepted, the couple usually go together to buy the ring.

It used to be traditional for just the woman to receive a ring, but now it is more usual for the couple to exchange rings and both make an equal spoken commitment (see The Ceremony, page 130).

🔔 **Not many people know that ...**

- The tradition of ring-giving dates back to Roman times when a ring, symbolising the couple's unending commitment, was given when they were betrothed.

- It is thought that, once put on, it should be taken off only in exceptional circumstances or the commitment would be broken. (A more practical reason is that your ring is much less likely to be lost or stolen if you wear it all the time!)

- It was the early Christians who made the ring-giving part of the wedding ceremony. The ring is now the symbol of marriage itself.

- In the Middle Ages the husband put a wedding ring on his wife's finger to ward off evil spirits.

🔔 Good luck – and bad

- For good luck the bride should glance in the mirror just before leaving the house for the ceremony. But she must not go back and look again or bad luck will befall her.

- You don't see many chimney sweeps these days, but get a glimpse of one on the wedding day and the best luck will be yours. You can hire one to stand outside the ceremony venue as you arrive, just to make sure!

- Other good omens are seeing a rainbow, spider, black cat, lamb or toad (but I don't recommend you hire a toad to sit outside the church!).

- Bad omens, on the other hand, include seeing a pig, an open grave or a lizard and hearing a cockerel crow after dawn. Monks and nuns are also bad news, being a sign that the couple will have to depend on charity to survive.

- In Scotland, it is thought that if a bride walks in the sun at the church on her wedding day, she will have good fortune and fertility. No problem – except she must also walk from east to west on the south side of the church and then circle the church three times.

- Bad weather on the way to the wedding in the UK is thought to be an omen of an unhappy marriage, but in countries where rain is often needed but not forthcoming, like Africa, rain is considered a good omen!

- There is an old saying that says stormy weather breeds a stormy marriage. Snow, on the other hand, is a sign that the couple will be blessed with fertility and wealth.
- Many people say it's traditional for the bride to be late for the ceremony but, in fact, it's supposed to be bad luck!

Transport

At formal weddings, it's usual to provide special cars to take the bride's mother and the attendants to the ceremony, and one for the bride and her father. If you live very near the ceremony venue, one car may be able to drive the bride's mother and attendants, then come back for the bride and her father. Cars will also be needed to take the bride and groom, the bride's parents and the bridesmaids to the reception (unless they are travelling with the best man or their own parents).

Your choice of transport depends on your finances, your dreams, the time of year and any special interests. You can have a Rolls-Royce, limousine, vintage or veteran car, pony and trap, horses and carriage, motorbike – it's your call! If you want something unusual, and you don't have personal contacts, spend some time well in advance researching. Costs can vary enormously – especially if the vehicles have to travel a long way before they reach you (a bit like taxis).

✂£ **Transport**

- You don't have to hire official cars at all – use your own, decorated with ribbons (preferably cleaned and valeted too!).
- Choose a reception within walking distance of the ceremony.

When you book the transport, make sure the firm has back-up vehicles in case of breakdowns or any other emergency. Confirm *in writing* the pick-up address, venue addresses, times, dates and number of journeys. If it matters to you, make sure the chauffeur wears a uniform. Find out if ribbons and flowers are provided for the vehicles. Pay the deposit in advance and arrange final payment details. Bear in mind a few practical facts:

- The larger your dress, the more room you'll need, in order not to get it crumpled.
- If all the bridesmaids are travelling in one official car, it must be big enough to accommodate them!
- If the wedding is in the middle of winter, a pony and trap may not offer much protection against the elements.
- Open-air transport will play havoc with your hairstyle – and if you choose a motorbike and sidecar you'll have to wear a helmet when travelling!

The photographs

This is one area that it's very important you get right because it's the one that provides the really lasting mementoes that you will treasure. Even if it's second time around for the bride and groom, don't be tempted to cut corners, and don't rely on guests to provide you with the perfect shot – the chances are they won't. So get a good photographer and ask him or her to take lots of pictures. When my husband and I got married, we decided we didn't want a picture of all the guests together – it seemed so cheesy at the time and always takes ages to get everyone organised. In our defence, we had been to rather a lot of weddings at the time, getting very fed up waiting around for the photographs after the ceremony. Now, of course, we regret it because we (or I in particular) would love to look back now and remember everyone who was with us.

You need to book your photographer (and videographer if you're having one) well in advance. Be warned: the best get booked up very early indeed. You can find lots listed in _Yellow Pages_ but it's more advisable to ask around your friends and family – word of mouth is the best recommendation.

It may be that someone in your family is a keen photographer and wants to take on the job. However, this is not really a good idea unless you are desperate to save money. Firstly, they won't be able to enjoy the day much if they have to take all the formal photographs. And secondly, if they aren't actually a professional, the results may be disappointing. It might be better simply to ask their advice on what to look for when choosing who you should employ.

Spend time with your chosen photographer, discussing what you want. If you decide to go the whole hog, you can have photographs taken before, during and after the ceremony, as well as at the reception. Obviously this will take up most of the day and probably the evening, too, and the price will reflect that. If you want to keep costs down, you can book your photographer for a specific time – say an hour and a half – and ask him to take a specific number of photographs. Tell him or her if you want them to be made up of formal, posed shots or a selection of more spontaneous snaps of your guests. If you don't, the photographer will do as they always do – and you may not be too happy with what that may involve. Ideally, make a list of the pictures you want taken. Give a copy to the best man so that he can check that you've got photos of everyone you wanted.

☺ **Ease the boredom**
If the weather is not co-operating – cold, wet or very hot – try to resist keeping your guests hanging around while you have dozens of photos taken. Have just a few taken at the church or outside the ceremony, then have more taken at the reception after people have been refreshed with a drink.

You should find out in advance whether the minister or registrar allows photographs inside the church or register office.

If you are unsure about the quality of local photographers, contact the British Institute of Professional Photography (see page 189), who will send you a list of registered members.

It is likely that lots of your guests will have video cameras at the wedding, so, if you know someone who is good with theirs and will be able to edit it for you as well, it would be much cheaper than an official one. However, the same caveats apply as to amateur photographers. If you do want to get a professional, shop around, prices do vary.

✂£ Taking your own photographs

Despite what I've said earlier, it is possible to do without an official photographer – as long as you are very organised and make arrangements in advance.

- Decide what poses you want and ask the best man and ushers to put everyone in place.
- Don't rely on just one camera; arrange for several friends (preferably some with digital cameras) to take the photos. Offer to pay for film, etc., if necessary.
- Choose some from each of them for your 'offical' set'. Have copies printed and mount them in albums.

Telling the world

You can, if you wish, put a notice in a newspaper, announcing your wedding. This may take the form of an informal announcement in a local paper, stating the date, time and venue of the ceremony, and may include an invitation to the ceremony for friends who live nearby. Ideally, it should come out a few days, or a week at most, before the day. Check the newspaper's deadline for copy. This is usually a few days or up to a week before the day that the paper is due to be published. The notice should be clearly and simply worded:

Mr and Mrs John Day are delighted to announce the marriage of their daughter Susan Anne to Mr Peter Andrew Blake at 12.30 pm on Saturday 26 February at St Andrew's Church, Whitetown. All friends are welcome at the church.

Alternatively, you may wish to put your announcement in a national newspaper. This is done as soon as you are engaged; it is much more formal (and more expensive) and the wording must adhere to a strict format. For example:

Mr DE Manson and
Miss LA Horton

The engagement is announced between David Edward, younger son of Colonel and Mrs Charles Manson of Oldbury, Berkshire, and Lucy Alexandra, daughter of Dr and Mrs William Horton of Exeham, Shropshire.

Those extra touches

Weddings are big business nowadays and there are literally dozens of extras available to give your day its finishing touches. On the small side, you can have printed matchbooks and napkins, personalised with the names of the bride and groom; helium balloons with or without messages on them, arranged to form everything from bunches to arches; ribbons everywhere; little shiny weddings bells, like confetti, scattered on the tables; tiny phials of bubbles on the tables (often given as a gifts to the men but in my opinion best blown by the children after the meal in front of the top table); tiny baskets of sweets, single flowers or lace handkerchiefs for the female guests; disposable cameras (these are intended for the guests to take pictures of each other during the reception but usually end up full of drunken mug-shots).

✄£ A favour to whom?

You don't have to give party favours so my advice is to forget all of them – many are pretty naff anyway! They're not going to make your day any more wonderful than it is already. As long as the room looks attractive with clean table linen, cutlery and crockery and a few flowers for colour, with tasty food and plenty to drink, the rest is immaterial. It's the people not the place that are most important!

If you're thinking big, you can have entertainment: a pianist, harpist or a string quartet to play tranquil music during the meal, a full steel band to get everyone dancing afterwards. You name it, it's available. There are hundreds of websites on the internet with loads of ideas. The only limitations are the bounds of your taste and finances. Some useful addresses are given at the back of this book.

🔔 **Sugared almonds**

Sugared almonds are a traditional wedding 'favour' for the ladies. Usually five sugared almonds (but sometimes other bon bons) are tied in a little piece of lace or embroidered material and put beside each place name or given out as guests leave. Ladies who are unable to attend are also sent one after the wedding from the bride. By the way, the ladies aren't supposed to eat the sweetmeats but save them as a keepsake.

The wedding present list

It is customary for guests to give a gift to the bride and groom to help them start their new life. Family members who cannot attend usually send a gift anyway. Friends unable to go are not expected to give one (unless they wish to).

If you are setting up home for the first time, then it makes sense to give people ideas of colours for linen, towels, table mats and so on, or specific sets you are collecting – like a particular make and style of dinner service, glassware or cutlery. Make sure your list includes all sorts of items, from very expensive to really cheap. It's not fair – in fact it's just greedy – to have nothing costing less than £50. Small kitchen utensils, glassware, which can be bought singly or in pairs, individual settings for a china dinner service and the extras like a gravy boat should be listed separately as well as bigger items.

You can make up a list yourself or organise it through a national department store or catalogue chain. The lists are usually available online as well as personally at the store but do remind guests to inform the store when they make their purchase so that the store can delete each item from the list as it is bought.

It is of course not compulsory to buy from a list and it is very acceptable – and, I think, much more personal – for guests to give something of their own choosing, especially if it reflects a particular interest or talent of their own.

Many people don't like giving money, but nowadays, particularly if the couple have already been together for years, they may ask for money or gift vouchers so that they can put them towards something large that they want.

Gifts are normally sent to the bride's parents, ready to be displayed on the day. If the bride and groom already live together, the gifts may be sent to them direct.

☺ **Be sure – insure!**
You may have a lot of valuable gifts coming in to your home before the wedding. Check with your house contents insurance company that they are covered. Most companies will include this if they have been notified in advance, but some may ask for a small additional premium. It is worth it though!

Chapter 5

Your At-a-glance Checklist

The last few chapters have contained a huge number of things that need to be done at various stages when you are planning and preparing for your wedding. This chapter puts them all together in one checklist. I suggest you tick each one off as it is done – whoever does it.

I have tried to arrange them roughly chronologically order, but there really isn't a precise order and in some cases things need to be done almost simultaneously!

As soon as you decide to get married
- Set the date
- Contact religious leader and/or registrar
- Fill in and submit official forms for licences etc.
- Make a guest list
- Book venue for ceremony
- Book reception venue, if separate
- Organise caterers if necessary
- Choose attendants
- Start thinking about outfits

Six months ahead
- Plan ceremony
- Choose bride's dress/ bridesmaids' dresses
- Arrange and meet dressmaker, if appropriate
- Book honeymoon, if going away
- Book any entertainment (e.g. for evening party)
- Choose and order cake, or arrange to have one made and decorated
- Book photographer and videographer
- Book official cars
- Apply for passport in new name, if preferred

Three months ahead
- Choose and order printed wedding stationery
- Select present list or information about presents and arrange with store, if necessary
- Buy bride's going-away outfit
- Order flowers
- Buy rings
- Order any hired outfits
- Buy any remaining accessories (e.g. shoes)

Six weeks ahead
- Print copies of maps and information about travel and local hotel/B & B accommodation
- Send out invitations, wedding present lists, maps, etc.

- Buy presents for attendants, parents, etc.
- Book hairdresser for the wedding day (plus a 'practice session', if necessary)
- Book any other beauty treatments for week of wedding, e.g. manicure, massage, waxing, etc.

One month before
- Notify caterers of numbers
- Confirm all arrangements with venues, minister or registrar, florist, photographer, etc.

Two weeks ahead
- Confirm numbers, if necessary, for ceremony and reception
- Give final numbers to caterers, with any menu details etc., if separate
- Make seating plan, if required

One week ahead
- Put an announcement in the local paper
- Check any tickets etc. for the honeymoon have arrived
- Make sure new passport has arrived, if necessary
- Hold rehearsal for ceremony
- Have final try-on of outfits in case any alternations are necessary.

Chapter 6

The Last Nights of Freedom

It is customary for the bride and groom to have separate hen and stag parties. The most important thing is to hold them at least 48 hours before the wedding. Anything less is guaranteed to spoil your wedding day! Hangovers and solemn vows (except for saying you'll never touch a drop again) don't go together. Ideally, plan your parties for the week before the wedding, to give yourselves plenty of time to recover.

To make sure the events are a success, don't leave everything until the last minute and do make sure you book it all down to the last detail. I once went to a hen night where we were supposed to be going to a club where a live group was playing. We all arrived only to discover it was ticket-in-advance only, so we ended up at the local Chinese restaurant instead!

There was a time when a night out with a few good mates was considered enough but many people nowadays seem to want more than that. Some spend hundreds per person on a fantastic spree. Stag and hen dos are big business these days.

It used to be the bride or groom who organised her or his

own party but now it's usually the chief bridesmaid or best man who plans it – including any little extra touches! It's best to consult the bride or groom as to what they'd like to do (unless it really is all supposed to be a complete surprise) and to talk with the other members of the party. Remember, if older folk are invited (mums or dads, for instance), make sure what you do is not going to be beyond them in terms of taste or physical exertion. A lap-dancer might thrill one prospective father-in-law but could be the death of another!

Traditionally, stags would go on a pub crawl, get legless, leave the groom tied naked to a lamppost and then retreat, ill. For girls, it was an Ann Summers-type party with booze and chocolates and loads of innuendo. Boring.

These days you can choose a complete package-holiday weekend specially designed for blokes or girls: and there are plenty of ideas to choose from.

In Nottingham, for instance (courtesy of Nottingham Activity Weekends at www.activity-weekends.co.uk), hens can have Maid Marion's Choice of clay pigeon shooting followed by a pamper day at a health spa for around £65 a head plus £30–£55 for hotel or B & B; stags can try Friar Tuck's Choice of quadbiking plus paintballing for around £55 plus similar accommodation costs.

At www.hitched.co.uk they're offering all sorts of zany weekends from around £195 per person. You can plan exactly what you want.

If you would rather plan something yourself, you could book first-class tickets on Eurostar to Paris (they often do a cheap day package), leaving fairly early in the morning, breakfast included on board. Do all the touristy things like the Eiffel Tower, Montmartre and the Sacré Coeur, Notre Dame, lunch in the Latin Quarter, rounding off the culture with perhaps a visit to the Mona Lisa at the Louvre (but not on a Tuesday – it's shut!). Then get a train back at about 8 pm from Paris and have Champagne and dinner (included) on the way home. If you don't live in London, you'd have to book accommodation for the night before and after, or you could stay overnight in Paris. Details of packages are available through Eurostar.

Other ideas for trips further afield could be Champagne-tasting in Reims, France, chocolate-tasting in Brussels or whisky-tasting at a distillery in the Scottish Highlands.

Closer to home, you could sample the white-knuckle rides on the three rollercoasters of the North – Nemesis at Alton Towers, the Ultimate at Lightwater Valley and The Big One at Blackpool Pleasure Beach. This and loads more ideas are available from www.confetti.co.uk.

If your budget – or your courage – doesn't go that far, you girls could try a traditional girls' night in. Buy some really luxurious manicure and pedicure products, face masks, perhaps even a mini jacuzzi (you can get some really cheap ones that fit in an ordinary bath). Get everyone round in PJs or dressing gowns. Have lots of sparkling wine or cocktails, favourite nibbles – exotic fruit, oysters, Belgian truffles, the lot – choose some chick flicks on DVD or video and you've got a great party!

🔔 **The stag tradition**

Stag nights have been going on right back to mediaeval times and have always been raucous affairs. The men – even in those days – gathered together, drunk loads, got very rowdy, sung bawdily and threw drinking vessels and plates in the hearth. The noise was to drive away the evil spirits who would be gathering to try to thwart the couple's 'rite of passage' on their wedding day (the leaving one life as single people for a new life as a married couple).

For the blokes, the manicure thing might not go down so well but there are still lots of cheaper options. I liked an idea on www.hitched.co.uk called Pub Golf. You plan a route of 9 (or 18!!) pubs. Decide in advance a handicap for each pub – 1, 2, 3, 4 or 5 – these equate to gulps of drink. At each one, each stag has to down a drink in the designated number of gulps, or less. If not, he forfeits a shot at the next pub so has to down his drink in one less. (When I first read this, I thought the shots were whole drinks and you had to down that number of drinks every time but I don't think many would last the distance that way!) Remember to eat plenty of food on the way round – and end up with a huge curry and loads of water before you go to bed!

If you're planning just a day-trip or evening do, here's a step-by-step guide to getting it right:

● Make a list of friends to invite – checking first with the bride or groom.

● Once you know who's going to be involved, choose the type of party or activity that would suit the people – not the other way round.

● Choose a venue that's easy for everyone to get to.

● Make provisional bookings at one or more venues (depending on the plan). If you're holding it at someone's house, start planning food, drink, etc.

● Tell everyone in advance of any theme and any equipment or special clothing they may need to bring. Make sure everyone knows how much it's going to cost and how and when they will have to pay.

● Make a list of who is definitely coming.

● Arrange any special 'surprises', such as a stripagram (look in *Yellow Pages* under Kissograms or visit www.stripagrams.co.uk). You can find loads of novelties under 'Party goods' in *Yellow Pages* or go to a website such as www.partydomain.co.uk or www.partysuperstores.co.uk.

● Confirm the booking and party numbers with any establishment (in writing if it involves accommodation or special preparations). Confirm again the day before the event by phone.

- Arrange a place to meet on the day and make sure everyone knows exactly where it is and what time you're starting.
- Make sure everyone has mobile phone numbers and/or contact names and numbers, including that of any venue. This is especially important if people are meeting at a venue or going on some sort of crawl, when stragglers can get lost. If you can contact each other, it shouldn't go far wrong.
- Arrange transport home. Book taxis in advance. Make sure no one drinks and drives.
- Intersperse your drinking with the odd glass of water – it does wonders for reducing the hangover.

Chapter 7

The Ceremony

Whether religious or civil, the ceremony will be bounded on all sides by customs and laws. You will obviously discuss your plans in detail with your minister or the superintendent registrar. Both will have loads of anecdotal information on what works and what doesn't!

This chapter offers some guidelines to point you in the right direction with a bit of help re the music, order of events and seating arrangements. Planning is all-important to make sure the whole thing runs smoothly. A rehearsal for all the main players is also a very good idea indeed, when it can be arranged. It takes away many of the anxious feelings on the day as you'll all know what's expected of you. Check with your minister or the registrar to see if this is possible.

Church services

If you are having a church service, the minister will guide you through your choices of service. This can be:

- The service in *The Book of Common Prayer* of 1662 (traditional service)
- The Series One service (alternative service, 1966)

● The Common Worship service (marriage service, 2000)
Copies of the Series One service or the Common Worship service can be obtained from The Church House Bookshop (see page 189).

> 🔔 **Confetti**
> *Confetti* is the Italian word for 'sweets'. In Italy, traditionally, sugared almonds were thrown over the couple as they left the church to symbolise prosperity and fertility. Nowadays, often, as here, paper confetti or real flower petals are used instead. In other countries the tradition of throwing rice or other grains has the same symbolism.

Once you have decided which service you want, the minister will probably ask you to meet him (or her) to go through the ceremony, discuss the words and vows and their significance. There are quite a lot of decisions to be made.
● You may want the service to include Holy Communion or Mass (usually only if you are both practising Christians).
● Choose the hymns and music.
● Decide if you want the choir and/or bells rung, and agree costs.
● Choose readings and decide on appropriate readers.
● Agree if the minister is going to give an address.
● Discuss the flowers and when it is appropriate to decorate the church.

- Ask if photography and video recording are allowed during the ceremony. If so, agree where and how this is to be done.
- Check if confetti is allowed in the churchyard. Most ministers will say 'No' to paper confetti but are happy if it is made of rice paper or real flower petals or rice.

🔔 **Ding, dong, bell**

The ringing of the bells after the ceremony isn't just a sign of celebration. It stems from the days when it was believed that the clanging bells would drive away any malicious demons wanting to ruin the newlyweds' future.

Who sits where

The traditional arrangement below applies to civil ceremonies too.

Altar or table

Left-hand side	Right-hand side
Bride's mother (and, later, father)	Groom and best man
Bride's siblings (if not part of the official wedding party)	Groom's parents and siblings (if not part of the official wedding party)
Bride's family	Groom's family
Bride's friends	Groom's friends

Special seating arrangements

If you have any disabled guests in wheelchairs, make sure they can sit where they have a good view but don't feel awkward.

If the bride's parents are divorced, discuss the seating arrangements in advance. If there is still animosity between them, it is usual for the bride's mother to sit in the front row with her new partner (if she has one), with the bride's father and his new partner (if he has one) in the row behind. If relations between them are more amicable, and neither or only one has a new partner, it is better if they all sit together in the front pew. However, there are no hard-and-fast rules: the best thing is to ask everyone involved and then agree something that the parents and the bride and groom are comfortable with.

🔔 **Bride on the left ...**

It's traditional for the bride's family to sit on one side whilst the groom's family sits on the other. This dates back to ancient times when tribes would end a feud by the daughter of one tribal leader being offered to the other tribe as a peace offering. The tribes were kept well apart during the handing-over ceremony to prevent any further fighting!

If the groom's parents are divorced, the groom's mother with her new partner (if she has one) should sit in the second row behind the groom and best man, with the groom's father (and his new partner if he has one) in the row behind. If neither or only one has a new partner and they all get on well, it is better if they all sit together in the second row. As ever, the most important thing is that everyone is comfortable with the arrangements.

The wedding party – who stands where
During the ceremony, the guests all stand in the pews, either side of the aisle.

The wedding party will be standing in the centre front as below:

Minister

Bride   Groom

Father of bride   Best man

Chief bridesmaid

Other attendants

If you have flower girls, they walk in front of the bride, then when the bride and groom are standing together they either move to the sides or walk back behind the bride and groom to stand behind the chief bridesmaid.

If you have page boys holding the train, or tiny bridesmaids, they walk behind the bride. When the procession comes to a halt, the chief bridesmaid should step forward to take the bride's bouquet and then remain behind her. The pages and tiny bridesmaids move back (or sit down with parents if they prefer).

🔔 **Sword at the ready**

The tradition of the bride standing on the left dates back to times when a knight would always have his lady on his left, leaving his right hand – his sword hand – free to protect her if they were attacked.

The order of service

Your minister will talk you through the service exactly as it happens. But it's helpful to read it through in advance to familiarise yourselves with the proceedings. It's also a good idea to tell all the members of the wedding party what will be expected of them.

Before the service

The ushers should get to the church at least 30 minutes before the service is due to begin as guests will start to arrive soon after this. They hand out order of service sheets and see guests to their seats (see Who sits where, page 132).

The groom and best man should arrive early and may greet a few guests before taking up their places at the front.

The bride's mother should arrive next, with the attendants. They have photographs taken, the bride's mother goes into church and is escorted to her seat (front left-hand pew) while the attendants wait at the door until the bride and her father arrive. If the minister is leading the procession into the church, he (or she) will remain at the door with them. If not, he will go into church to receive the procession at the chancel steps.

♤ Rights and lefts

- The right hand is a symbol of strength, resource and purpose. The bride and groom hold each other's right hand during the ceremony to signify that they can depend on each other and their marriage, and that they should go forward with great resourcefulness and determination. The joining of hands also symbolises the merging of two lives into one.
- The Romans started the tradition of putting the ring on the third finger of the left hand. They believed that that finger was connected directly to the heart by 'the vein of love' (vena amoris).

The service starts

The bride and her father arrive. Pre-wedding photographs are taken. The wedding party assembles in the order they will walk down the aisle.

🔔 Rings and things

- Puritans in the seventeenth century thought any ring was a sign of vanity so tried to have wedding rings abolished. They didn't succeed but it's thought that they found it more acceptable to have a plain gold wedding band, rather than an ornate ring, and that tradition has remained to this day.

- Also in the late seventeenth century, it became stylish to have the wedding ring put on the third finger of the left hand during the ceremony but then to wear it on the thumb afterwards. Funnily enough, that tradition didn't last!

- The Maoris of New Zealand have rings of carved bone or greenstone. They are known as 'infinity loops', representing never-ending love.

- It is customary for the groom to kiss the bride after the ceremony. This dates back to the time when a kiss on the cheek was a sign of acceptance of a contract.

A signal is given to the organist or person in charge of the music. The groom and best man stand up and move in front of the chancel steps on the right of the aisle. The congregation stands up. The processional march or hymn starts and the bridal party walks slowly down the aisle.

The bride stands to the left of the groom with her father slightly behind her on her left. The chief bridesmaid steps forward and takes the bride's bouquet. If the bride has a veil, the chief bridesmaid or the bride's father will help her lift it off her face (or it can remain down until after they are pronounced husband and wife). The first hymn is sung (unless there was a processional hymn) and there may be a reading.

The ceremony begins. The minister explains the significance of marriage and asks anyone to declare if there is a reason why the couple shouldn't marry (slight pause). He (or she) will then ask who gives the bride in marriage.

The bride's father takes her right hand and passes it to the minister who then passes it to the groom, who takes it in his right hand. The father then steps back.

The couple make their vows according to which service they have chosen. At the given moment, the best man puts the rings on the minister's prayer book for them to be blessed.

The rings are then exchanged and the couple are pronounced husband and wife. The best man and the bride's father take their seats. If the bride hasn't lifted her veil before, she does so now, with the help of the groom.

A hymn may be sung. The bride and groom follow the minister to the altar for prayers. He may now give an address. Another hymn is sung, then the final blessing is given.

The wedding party go to the vestry to sign the register in front of two witnesses (usually chosen from the wedding party). There is often an instrumental or vocal recital while this happens.

After the signing, a rousing anthem is played and the bride and groom lead everyone out of the church.

The music

Before you decide what music and hymns you want, check with the minister whether you have to book the organist and if there is a fee. Some churches use taped music and others have a piano instead. This will, obviously, make a difference to your choice of music. You may have a musician amongst your friends or family who will play for you for the whole service or sing or play before the service and/or during the signing of the register. You may want to book professional musicians to perform during the ceremony.

☺ **Choirs aren't always heavenly!**

Choirs are only as good as the parishioners who choose to join them. They all work extremely hard – most attend practice every week – but not everyone who chooses to sing has the voice of an angel. When we were planning to get married in my family church, the vicar tentatively asked us if we had our hearts set on a choir. He looked very relieved when we said we hadn't even thought of it because, in his words, 'They are very enthusiastic but really not quite up to it!'

Check if there is a choir (it's a good idea – if they are up to it – to have them to boost the hymn-singing, especially nowadays when many people do not attend church regularly). Find out how much they charge and decide if you want them to proceed down the aisle before you with the minister or to be in the choir stalls before you begin.

You can have some secular songs or music during the ceremony, but you must agree this with your minister.

You will need music at several points during the service and it is a good idea to try to choose pieces that match the mood at each stage. Here are some suggestions:

Before the service
For this, you want something joyful that anticipates the celebration to come.
Handel, *Coro* from *Water Music*
Handel, *Hornpipe in D* from *Water Music*
Beethoven, *Für Elise*
Debussy, Arabesque No. 1 from *Deux Arabesques*
Purcell, *Trumpet Tune*
Elgar, *Nimrod* from *Enigma Variations*
Beethoven, *Ode to Joy*

Alternatively you could have a lighter piece, such as *Greensleeves*.

For the bridal procession
Choose something stately and inspiring that the bride can walk
to slowly and majestically. Practise beforehand if you can – this
will stop you trying to hurry!
Bliss, *A Wedding Fanfare*
Boyce, *Trumpet Voluntary*
Mozart, *Wedding March* from *The Marriage of Figaro*
Purcell, *Fanfare*
Handel, *Arrival of the Queen of Sheba*
Wesley, *Choral Song*
Mendelssohn, Sonata No. 3, first movement
Wagner, *Bridal Chorus* from *Lohengrin* 'Here Comes the Bride'
Elgar, *Pomp and Circumstance March*
Clarke, *Trumpet Voluntary*

You may prefer that the choir and congregation stand and
sing a processional hymn as you walk down the aisle. Again,
keep the mood joyful. These are good examples of suitable
hymns:

All People That On Earth Do Dwell
Praise My Soul The King Of Heaven
Love Divine All Loves Excelling
Oh Jesus I Have Promised

The hymns I've listed so far could be used during the service if not for the procession; you'll need at least one more after the prayers and final blessing. There is often one after the vows as the bride and groom move forward to the altar for prayers too. Choose your favourites, but do check with your minister that they are appropriate – Fight The Good Fight and Onward Christian Soldiers may be your favourites, but they're not really suitable in this case! Some popular ones are:

All Things Bright And Beautiful
Morning Has Broken
Lord Of The Dance
Now Thank We All Our God
O Perfect Love
Give Me Joy In My Heart
Immortal, Invisible
Make Me A Channel Of Your Peace

You may also choose a sung or spoken psalm after the reading. Your minister will advise on the most appropriate.

During the signing of the register
You may like to have a soloist musician or vocalist or a group to sing or play while the bride and groom sign the register. The list opposite contains some popular classics but you may want to choose something more modern. Again you can have what you like, providing the minister agrees. He or she will be happy to offer advice and copies of hymn books for you to look through.

☺ **Listen to the lyric**
Think about the words – especially if you choose a modern secular song. They aren't always as appropriate as they first seem by the opening lines. Something like The Beatles' 'All You Need Is Love' works well but 'Band of Gold', despite sounding perfect, actually contains the words, *'Now that you're gone, all that's left is a band of gold…'!*

Bach, *Jesu, Joy of Man's Desiring*
Bach, *Ave Maria*
Franck, *Panis Angelicus*
Schubert, *Ave Maria*
Mozart, *Laudate Dominum*
Bach, *Air on a G string*
Albinoni, *Adagio in G minor*
Bach, *Choral Prelude*
Mozart, Romanze from *Eine Kleine Nachtmusik*
Borodin, Nocturne from *String Quartet*
Mendelssohn, Nocturne from *A Midsummer Night's Dream*
Saint-Saëns, *Bénédiction Nuptiale*

At the end of the ceremony
As the bride and groom lead everyone out of church, a rousing celebratory piece is usually played.

Wagner, Wedding March from *Lohengrin*
Mendelssohn, Wedding March from *A Midsummer Night's Dream*
Verdi, Grand March from *Aida*
Widor, Toccata from Symphony No. 5 in F
Handel, *Music for the Royal Fireworks*
Bach, *Prelude and Fugue in A*
Clarke, *Trumpet Voluntary*
Greig, *Triumphal March,* Opus 53 No. 3

Copyright

Copyright exists for 70 years after the death of the writer of hymns or music, so if you want to reprint the words of a modern hymn in your order of service sheets, you may need to get permission from the copyright holder. This can be obtained for a small fee (look in the front of the publication you are copying from). However, you don't need permission to sing the hymns, and so, strangely, if hymn books are being used, that's acceptable. Ask your minister for further advice.

🔔 **Aloha**
The 'Hawaiian Wedding Song' that Elvis sings in the film *Blue Hawaii* really is sung at Hawaiian weddings!

Ceremonies of other denominations and beliefs

As you already know, you have to have a licence from the superintendent registrar before you can marry in any church other than a Church of England.

Roman Catholic ceremony

You may marry during a nuptial Mass if both of the couple are Roman Catholic. If only one is, the marriage would be celebrated without a Mass. The rites of marriage are the same.

The ceremony is similar to that of the Church of England, but the bride and groom have to promise to bring up any children in the Roman Catholic faith. Also they are asked if they consent to marry 'according to the rite of our Holy Mother the Church'. They then make their vows and exchange rings.

Nonconformist Church ceremony

This is very similar to the Church of England service, with slightly different wording according to the denomination. The ministers are usually authorised to perform marriages, so the registrar need not be present, but you should always check beforehand.

Quaker ceremony

Both the Society's registering officer and the superintendent registrar need to be notified of the wedding.

At the ceremony the couple usually sit surrounded by friends and family. Then, when they feel the time is right, they both stand and they both make declarations promising that through divine assistance they will be loving and faithful so long as they both live on Earth. They both sign the civil marriage certificate in front of the registrar and all the Society of Friends sign a Quaker certificate when the meeting is over.

🔔 **Get ahead!**

At a Russian Orthodox Church ceremony, the bride and groom have to stand on a special carpet to recite their vows but first they have to race each other to reach it. Whoever gets there first is supposed to be the ruler of the household!

Jewish ceremony

After you have notified the superintendent registrar, the marriage can take place anywhere. The couple stand under a canopy called a *chuppah*. This symbolises the time when the Israelites had to live in tents. Both sets of parents join the couple under the chuppah with the best man just behind and to the left of the bridegroom. Family and friends stand behind.

There is a short address by the rabbi, then the groom places a ring on the bride's finger and makes a declaration.

A reading and the signing of the Hebrew marriage contract follow, with both bride and groom making their promises to each other. They then sign a covenant, which is a proclamation of their vows.

Civil ceremonies

Whether you are getting married in a register office or another approved venue, the ceremony has civil vows with no religious content. You can choose appropriate readings, poems or music for the occasion, which you should discuss with the registrar.

If you are marrying in a register office, you must bear in mind two things:

The register office has limited space so you will only be able to have a small gathering to witness the actual ceremony (you can, of course, have as many people as you like to the reception afterwards).

It is more than likely there will be another wedding immediately after yours. The ceremony only lasts about 20 minutes so you haven't got much time for sentimentality!

As with a church wedding, it is important that the guests know what they are doing. It's a good idea to have at least one usher to show people where to go. You can have bridesmaids and a best man if you so wish (though many couples choose to have no attendants at all). It is also not compulsory for the bride to come in with her father. Many couples arrive together. The choice is yours.

The legalities and order of ceremony in an approved venue licensed for weddings are the same as for a register office. The difference is you can have as large or small a venue as you wish, so can have as elaborate or simple a ceremony as you wish. In other words, there is more scope for individuality than in a register office.

You will get lots of help from the proprietors about what you can or cannot have. It is worth knowing that the licence is granted for a room within the premises, not the whole property, so do make sure you ask to see the actual room where the ceremony will take place. You must choose only non-religious music, readings and poems to be interspersed during the ceremony, but these can be selected to make it as individual, memorable and romantic as you like. Make sure you check with the superintendent registrar that what you want is acceptable.

The seating arrangements are up to you. Many venues will arrange the chairs in a variety of ways, to suit your preferences. As for who sits where, in my experience, everyone feels more comfortable if you follow similar 'rules' as for a church wedding (see page 132).

Music

It is a good idea to have music playing to fill the gaps during the ceremony. Your guests will feel a lot more relaxed if there is music playing while they are waiting for the bride and groom to enter, and also at moments of silence during the proceedings. You can't have religious music at a civil ceremony, but there are lots of compilation CDs of wedding music available. You may choose anything that is special to you – even a selection of modern love songs or ballads. As you will be playing music in a public place, check with the proprietors that they have a suitable licence, so you don't have to worry about copyright (but there shouldn't be any problem at all). Many venues will also provide a CD player and perhaps someone to operate it.

☺ **Strike the right note**
It is a good idea to pre-record your choices of music in the correct order on to one CD, so that whoever is in charge of the music can't get confused!

Poems and readings
You can also have a poem or a reading – although, again, this can't be from a religious source or refer in any way to religious subjects. Because there is no standard format, you can ask one or two friends or relatives to select their own pieces to read, or you and your partner can choose ones that would mean something special to you. They don't have to be soppily romantic; they can be humorous, traditional, pearls of ancient wisdom or even odes written especially for the occasion.

Here are a couple of my favourites, just to get your mind working.

Love Lives Beyond
Love lives beyond
The tomb, the earth, which fades like dew!
I love the fond,
The faithful, and the true.
Love lives in sleep,
The happiness of healthy dreams:
Eve's dews may weep
But love delightful seems.
'Tis seen in flowers,
And in the morning's pearly dew;
In earth's green hours,
And in the heaven's eternal blue.
'Tis heard in spring
When light and sunbeams, warm and kind,
On angel's wing
Bring love and music to the mind.
And where is voice,
So young, so beautiful, and sweet
As nature's choice,
Where spring and lovers meet?
Love lives beyond
The tomb, the earth, the flowers, and dew.
I love the fond,
The faithful, young, and true.

John Clare

The Art of a Good Marriage
(This is a shortened version)

A good marriage must be created.
In marriage the little things are the big things ...
It is never being too old to hold hands,
It is remembering to say 'I love you' at least once a day,
It is never going to sleep angry,
It is having a mutual sense of values and common objectives,
It is standing together and facing the world,
It is forming a circle of love that gathers in the whole family,
It is speaking words of appreciation and demonstrating
gratitude in thoughtful ways,
It is having the capacity to forgive and forget,
It is giving each other an atmosphere in which each can grow,
It is a common search for the good and the beautiful,
It is not only marrying the right person, it is being the right
partner.

Wilfred Peterson

The order of ceremony
Guests should arrive at least 10 minutes before the ceremony is
due to start. They may be able to go straight in, or have to wait
in a reception room until another wedding has finished.

The bride and groom must meet the superintendent
registrar immediately beforehand, to complete the

documentation. They may do this together or separately.

The couple may enter together or, as in a church ceremony, the groom may go in and wait at the front. The bride then enters, possibly accompanied by her father.

The couple stand before the superintendent registrar in front of their friends and family.

The wording of the ceremony may vary but it must follow a format approved by the registrar. First the couple must state that there is no legal reason why they should not marry. They are reminded of the solemn and binding nature of the vows they are about to take. Then they repeat their vows after the registrar.

Rings are exchanged, the couple are pronounced husband and wife and then the documents are signed in front of two official witnesses.

Music can be played as the bride and groom leave, with their guests following.

🔔 **Party on**

A Bedouin wedding used to last a week, but now it's more like two days. It is considered the combining of two families, not just two people. The couple don't meet before the wedding celebrations are complete, when the bride walks into her new husband's house and her new husband is waiting for her.

☺ **Don't leave your guests guessing!**

If you're having a non-traditional ceremony, do make sure your guests know exactly what to expect. It's very important that they are shown or told what to do when they arrive.

At a wedding we went to recently we arrived too early to go into the room where the ceremony was being held, so we went into the bar with numerous other guests. When the bride pulled up outside, we had to rush into the ceremony room ahead of her. There was no one to tell us where to sit, no order of ceremony – nothing. As we all scuttled in and sat down in the nearest seats, my aunt immediately started fussing because we were the groom's relatives, and so should have been sitting on the right, not the left. Everyone was looking around anxiously, not knowing where to sit or what to do. Then without any warning or change of music, the bride arrived, swept down to the front with her bridesmaids in hot pursuit and the ceremony began. Fortunately, the registrar was very pleasant and told us when to stand and sit but even the wedding party forgot that there was supposed to be a reading. It was only remembered at the end, and was delivered with some embarrassment, just as the bride and groom were about to rush out again. I found it all rather disconcerting and disappointing.

After the ceremony

Photographs are usually taken outside the church or ceremony room. Think about this when you choose your venue – many churches and some licensed premises have beautiful gardens or ancient buildings that make perfect backdrops for your wedding pictures, but register offices are often not terribly attractive, so you may want to wait until you get to your reception venue for the majority of the photographs. As I've said before, if the weather's not good – or even just because you know a lot of your guests have travelled a long way to get to the wedding – it might be better to just have a few taken now of the official wedding party and then more taken at the start of the reception, when the guests have had, at least, a little refreshment.

Ceremonies abroad

Whether you dream of a wedding on a tropical island, in a romantic city, floating in a hot-air balloon or at an Elvis-style ceremony in Las Vegas, it can be arranged. You can buy packages, organised by reputable travel companies, which will take care of the entire thing – all you have to do is turn up.

Sometimes the couple take a few close family members and friends to enjoy the day (the trouble is, that means having them on honeymoon with you!).

For a complete guide, get a copy of *Getting Married Abroad* by Amanda Statham (published by W. Foulsham & Co. Ltd).

Before you start booking, here are a few words of warning. There are tour operators around that are not very reputable so do check everything out before you sign on the dotted line. Check that the company itself is registered with ABTA or ATOL – this will, at least, protect the holiday itself. Also, if looking at internet sites, I don't advise you to contact them unless there is a registered address displayed, and don't give credit card or other personal details unless it is a secure site (you should see a little padlock icon on the bottom right of your screen). Don't part with any money until you are absolutely sure everything is bona fide.

⌂ **Horseshoe for good luck**

It's customary for the bride to be given a horseshoe after the ceremony as a symbol of good luck. Romans thought that the U-shape protected them from evil, because they could escape through the break in the loop. In mediaeval times they believed that it symbolised the moon, which is the protector of women and also a symbol of fertility. Others believed that a shiny new horseshoe would keep witches away.

It is possible, but not easy, to make the arrangements yourselves – the problems of 'red tape' can be huge, and may include lengthy consultations with the authorities of the country where you intend to marry, as well as some very daunting lists of required documents.

Legalities vary from country to country and, if you do organise it yourself, you may even find that the marriage will not be recognised in the UK. However, if you go through a reputable agent and have a Christian or civil ceremony according to UK laws, you should be fine. But never just take the agent's word for it: check everything for yourselves with the consulate of the country.

Many well-known travel companies include wedding packages in their brochures. Alternatively, you could go to a specialist wedding company (see page 189).

Religious blessings

Some people who have strong religious beliefs are unable to marry in church because, for example, one of the couple is divorced. In this case, you may wish to have a blessing in church after you have been married in a register office or at another venue licensed to hold weddings. This can be held on the same day as the wedding or on a later date. You have to have been legally married first and will have to produce the marriage certificate to prove it. Talk to your minister, in advance, to arrange the timings.

The occasion can be as big or small as you like. You need no witnesses so it could be just the two of you with the minister. Alternatively, you may like to have close family and friends with you.

The service may contain your choice of readings, prayers and hymns, Holy Communion or a Mass, if appropriate, but you do not exchange vows.

Chapter 8
The Reception

As I've said earlier, you need to book the venue and any caterers well in advance.

☺ **The lawn will recover**

Don't be put off the idea of holding the reception in your garden, because you think it will ruin the lawn, or because of the time of year. I got married in February and had a large marquee taking up the entire garden. Not only did my father's lawn spring back to life in a matter of a couple of weeks but even the shallots, planted in January, survived having the matting laid over them!

The marquee was also heated so it didn't matter that it was cold outside. Guests were greeted in the front hallway of the house, then moved through the lounge, collecting their glasses of Champagne on the way, out through the patio doors, along a heated walkway, into the 'tent'.

First, draw up a guest list to decide the size of venue you need. If you're planning a formal meal followed by an evening party, choose a venue that can accommodate both. If you're having the ceremony at an authorised venue, then, obviously, it makes sense to hold the reception there too. If you're thinking of holding it at home, an average house can only accommodate around 40 guests comfortably. But if you have a large garden, a marquee is a brilliant idea. You can choose one with a lining that matches or tones with the colour of the bridesmaid's dresses and flowers, and rush matting or a wooden floor and, even, a dance area can be provided too.

The food

Obviously, if you are having the reception at a hotel or pub, they will arrange the catering at a fixed price per guest, which will vary according to whether you choose a sit-down, waiter-service meal, a self-service hot or cold table or a finger buffet. It can be as lavish or as simple as you like.

☺ **Get help!**
If the bride's parents are having the reception in their home and decide to do the actual catering themselves, hire help to do the serving of food and drinks on the day. All that's needed then is a supervisory eye on proceedings, so that they can enjoy the reception. This isn't any ordinary party where the host and hostess expect to be rushed off their feet – this is the sort of day that may only come once in a lifetime!

If you are having the reception in a hired hall, you can be very flexible about the style and type of food you have. And if it's at home, you can bring in caterers or do it yourself. But if you choose this last option, even if you involve most of the family it's worth remembering that the list of things to organise for any wedding is simply enormous, and if you have to plan the food, too, down to the last tomato, that really adds to the pressure.

The drinks

You are not obliged to pay for all your guests' drinks at the reception. It is best to decide on a budget for drinks and then arrange everything beforehand.

If you're having the reception in licensed premises, find out how much the drinks are going to cost because you will have to pay bar prices. If you are offering a 'free bar', this must be arranged in advance so that the bar staff can keep a tab. Guests can choose what they like up to a limit that you have fixed – although you can of course pay for everyone's drinks throughout the party. A ticket system is a good idea, especially if there is more than one reception going on, so you don't get charged for someone else's guests' drinks.

If you aren't having a 'free bar', you could supply drinks when guests arrive (usually sherry or sparkling wine or Buck's Fizz) and a glass of sparkling wine for the toast. Another option is to offer free drinks throughout the formal reception and a pay-bar at the evening party. Whatever your choice, agree the type of wines and number of bottles to be provided in advance so you know how much you will be paying for.

Always have plenty of soft drinks available too – fruit juice, jugs of sparkling and still water and cola or lemonade – especially if you have invited a large number of children.

Do make sure the wine you pay for is actually served to your guests. I have heard of weddings where the majority of guests have had very little wine offered to them but the bill has been enormous. Cunning wine waiters keep the formal wedding party 'topped up' so they are unaware that the other guests aren't getting much. For every bottle the waiters serve to the guests, they secrete one away for their own consumption later. (A couple I know avoided this by asking the waiting staff to keep all the empty bottles so that they could see exactly how much had been consumed – and they didn't ask until just before the reception started so the staff had to comply.)

If you are having the reception in a hall or at home, you will be able to buy the drinks at shop prices and possibly take advantage of special offers. Most large supermarkets and wine stores will offer 'sale or return' on large quantities, which means you can buy more than you think you'll need, to be on the safe side, and return any unopened bottles for a refund afterwards. You can also make use of discounts for cases of wine – usually 5 per cent. Most off-licences and supermarkets will also lend glasses. You simply leave a deposit, which will be returned if there are no breakages. (If you do have breakages, it is usually cheaper to replace the broken glasses with some from the supermarket than it is to lose the deposit.) Always check that the glasses are intact and clean when you collect them and check if you are expected to wash them before you return them.

☺ **Don't put the parson's nose out of joint!**
If you're having a religious ceremony, don't forget to invite the celebrant to the reception. Most refuse, but they all like to be asked.

Gifts galore

It is customary, when possible, to display the wedding presents at the reception. This is easy if the reception is at home but if you're in a public venue you will need to check the arrangements for their safe keeping. In some cases it may not be a good idea at all, so discuss it with the proprietors well in advance. If it seems it's not viable, you could display them in a private house and invite guests back to see them if they wish.

The gifts should be taken to the venue the day before or on the morning of the wedding and need to be kept securely (check that the venue's insurance covers this). Have them arranged on a table in a corner of the reception room, preferably nowhere near an entrance where an uninvited guest might pop in and help himself! Make sure you've listed who gave what beforehand but don't display the gift card with each present because some people feel embarrassed if they have given a more modest gift than others.

If people have given money, list their names (but not the amounts) on a card and display that.

If you had a wedding list, you shouldn't get too many duplicates but, as not everyone asks for a copy of the list, it does happen – we got four toasters and three ironing boards! The advantage of displaying them is that, with any luck, if people realise their present has been duplicated, they may insist on exchanging the gift for you.

You can write thank-you letters before the wedding, but most couples wait until after the day – so as not to tempt fate.

Make sure someone has been delegated to pack up the presents after the reception and arrange delivery to the couple's home after their honeymoon. This is usually one or both sets of parents but the best man and chief bridesmaid should offer to help.

Reception etiquette

The bride and groom will be the first to arrive at the reception, closely followed by both sets of parents. They then get ready to greet the guests.

The receiving line

At a formal reception, it is usual for the bride and groom and their parents to greet the other guests. The first person should be the bride's mother, then the bride's father, groom's mother, groom's father, bride and finally the groom. (If the best man gets to the reception in time, he can join the line after the groom, but he may be more use making sure the guests have a drink and are mingling comfortably.)

The guests are greeted by name if the bride's parents know them. If not, they are asked their names. They then move along the line greeting each member of the wedding party in turn. I have been to weddings where a toastmaster has been in charge of proceedings (which is great when it comes to the speeches) and has announced everyone as they arrive – this takes even longer and is, in my opinion, a bit over the top.

Getting all the guests through the line can be a lengthy process and so it is really important that they are well looked after once they've moved into the reception room. And if you have a very large number of guests, you might like to have a waiter or two offering trays of drinks to sustain them whilst they are queuing outside!

The seating plan

If you are having a sit-down meal, a seating plan is very important. There is nothing worse than a free-for-all with everyone grabbing seats and some poor people left not even being able to sit with their partners.

As soon as you have a list of all the guests who have accepted the invitation, start working out who would be best sitting with whom. It's usually the job of the bride and both mothers to deal with that headache!

The top table and families are usually seated according to the diagram below.

8	7	6	5	4	3	2	1

10	1 Chief bridesmaid	9
	2 Best man	
	3 Bride's father	
	4 Bride	
	5 Groom	
	6 Bride's mother	
	7 Groom's father	
	8 Groom's mother	
	9 Other attendants and bride's family	
	10 Other attendants and groom's family	

This arrangement is not set in stone. Some people move the bride and groom to (3) and (4) with the bride's father at (2) and groom's mother at (1), the bride's mother (5), groom's father (6), best man (7) and chief bridesmaid (8).

The family tables, (9) and (10), can be mixed as you wish. The closest family members should sit here and if there are little bridesmaids and pages who are not related to the bride or groom, they should be on these tables with their parents too. Alternatively, sit them at the tables nearest to the family tables.

If either set of parents is divorced, you will probably need to rearrange the seating. Hopefully, this can be worked out amicably. You could perhaps put new partners on the family tables, or have a bigger top table and put everyone there.

Other guests are arranged at separate tables. It's a good idea to mix people up so you don't have all the groom's friends together and all the bride's friends together. However, it's not a good idea to seat individuals with no one they know or to split couples – everyone should be able to enjoy the meal, not have to struggle to make small talk politely with people they don't know and don't want to know! Do remember to consider any family feuds and personal rifts – you have to take into account that Auntie Jean hasn't spoken to Uncle Rick in 20 years and that, since their divorce, Jude and Ben can hardly stand the sight of each other!

Remember, there are no rules that can't be broken. The most important thing is that everyone is happy with the arrangements and can enjoy the occasion. The one thing to avoid is any resentment.

🔔 **No need to tidy up**
In Estonia, after the wedding feast, the food is left on the table until dawn to feed wandering spirits and lost souls.

At the meal
If you have a toastmaster, he should announce the meal and direct guests to their seats. If not, the best man and ushers should be at hand to help people. Guests should make their way to their seats but remain standing.

The wedding party will then proceed to the top table in pairs, as follows:

Bride and groom, bride's father with groom's mother, bride's mother with groom's father, best man with chief bridesmaid.

(Younger bridesmaids and pageboys usually go their seats with their parents. Their part in the proceedings is over and they can enjoy themselves.)

The toastmaster (or best man) then calls upon the minister, if present, to say grace. If he isn't there and it has been a religious ceremony, the bride's father should do the honours.

The meal is then served, first to the bride and groom and the rest of top table. If it is self-service, the bride and groom should go first.

☺ **Eat up!**
A word to the bride and groom: no one should start to eat until you have started, and the waiting staff must wait for you to finish before starting to serve another course. So do remember to pick up your fork promptly at the beginning of the meal and don't sit with your soup spoon halfway to your mouth while your guests are desperate for their main course!

Cutting the cake
This is best done as soon as the meal is over. The toastmaster (or best man) calls for everyone's attention and the bride and groom place their hands on the knife and cut the cake together, to symbolise their shared future.

The bride holds the knife in her right hand (unless she's left-handed) and the groom places his right hand on top, then her other hand on top of his. (If the icing is very hard, he may need to add pressure from his other hand, too, but the knife only has to penetrate a little into the cake as a token gesture; they don't have to cut out a whole slice!)

🔔 Cakes and customs

- In Roman times the cake was part of the wedding ceremony. It was a plain dough of wheat flour, salt and water. It was broken into pieces and thrown over the bride as part of the fertility ritual and over the groom to symbolise prosperity in the future. In Scotland, oatcakes used to be crumbled in the same way.

- Some Native American tribes and the Fijians still incorporate the cake in the ceremony itself.

- The first fruit cake, as we know it, used to be called The Groom's Cake. It represented his fruitfulness and fertility. It was also supposed to bring luck to all who ate it. The bride had to cut the first slice with her husband's help otherwise they would remain childless.

- The modern three-tiered iced cake is thought to represent the spire of Saint Bride's Church in the City of London.

- If a bridesmaid sleeps with a piece of the wedding cake under her pillow she is supposed to dream of her future partner.

- In Bermuda it is traditional for the wedding cake to be decorated with a tiny sapling. The newlyweds plant the little tree outside their home and, as it grows, it symbolises their love growing stronger. (I don't want to think about what happens if it dies!)

There will usually be some more official photographs at this point, which can take a while. By now, the wine waiters should be pouring glasses of sparkling wine and soft drinks as appropriate for the toasts. When the cake has been cut, a caterer will whisk it away to be cut and then handed round while the speeches are being made. If you are having a large wedding and have prepared an extra tier of cake as I suggested on page 107, it can be cut up and put on platters in advance, ready to serve to the guests as soon as the 'real' cake is being cut.

If you prefer, the cake-cutting can be done after the speeches, but that then leaves a lull before the cake is produced when the formalities are all over.

🔔 **Have your cake and eat it!**

It is a wonderful tradition to save the top tier of the wedding cake ready for the first baby's christening or naming ceremony. Simply wrap it tightly in double-thickness greaseproof paper, then foil. Put it in an airtight container and store it in a cool, dark place. You can also seal it in a freezer-proof container and freeze it. When the time comes, simply chip off all the old marzipan and icing, lace it with a little brandy, then re-cover with marzipan and ice it. I kept my top tier for five years before my daughter was born and the cake was superb!

The speeches

After the cake-cutting, it's time for the speeches and thanks, starting with the bride's father, followed by the groom and finally the best man.

Three important tips for any speech-maker: keep it short; don't try to be funny unless you naturally are; and be sincere. The actual content is up to you, but there are a few conventions that it's as well to adhere to.

The bride's father should:

- Praise the bride.
- Include a few anecdotes about her past.
- Thank everyone involved in the organisation of the wedding.
- Propose a toast to the bride and groom.

The groom should:

- Thank his father-in-law for his good wishes.
- Thank the bride's parents for the wedding.
- Thank his parents and anyone else who has made a contribution towards the day.
- Thank the guests for coming and for their gifts and good wishes.
- Thank the ushers for their help.
- Thank the best man for his help and support.
- Make a comment about how lovely the bridesmaids look (and how smart any pageboys look) and propose a toast to the bridesmaids (and pageboys).

The groom may like to give out any gifts bought for the parents and attendants at the relevant points during his speech. But he may prefer to get his speech out the way, then make a special presentation to them after all the speeches are complete. Either way, he should decide beforehand and arrange, if necessary, for the toastmaster or best man to announce that the groom has a few more words he'd like to say after the best man's speech.

The best man should:

- Thank the groom on behalf of the bridesmaids and himself for inviting them to be part of the ceremony.
- Tell a few anecdotes about the groom's past (preferably not too risqué, in view of the mixed company!).
- Read out any telemessages or cards.

☺ **Vet the messages first!**
At our wedding, two old friends of my husband sent a rather suggestive message, signed 'from Whiplash Wilma and the Black Leather Queen'. My mum nearly had a fit!

If the bride likes, she can say a few words when the three formal speeches are over – it doesn't have to be pre-planned (I didn't intend to say anything but when it came to the time, it just seemed the right thing to do).

Delivering the speech

Anyone who is making a speech should have practised it thoroughly beforehand. I gave lots of hints for how to prepare your speech on pages 46–7, but here are a few more to help you through the actual ordeal on the day.

- Unless you are good at projecting your voice, use a microphone. Don't hold it too close to your mouth or it will scream and your voice will sound muffled. Before you start, say a few words to get the level right. (There's nothing wrong with that old chestnut, 'Can you hear me at the back?')

- Speak more slowly than when talking normally. Don't be afraid to pause and laugh where appropriate and respond to the guests if they react to what you're saying (which, hopefully, they will).

- Try to appear calm even if you're practically fainting with nerves. Don't fiddle with change in your pockets or keep shuffling the cue cards. The more nervous you appear, the more uncomfortable your audience will be, which in turn will affect you even more. If you look happy, everyone will relax.

- Think of the speech as just saying some nice things about the day – which is all it is.

- Don't drink much beforehand or you'll get befuddled (you need a clear head and can make up for it later!).

- Have a glass of water handy in case your mouth goes dry or you need a pause to gather your thoughts.

- Try to enjoy it. Once you start, it's not too bad, honestly!

The first dance

If there is dancing at the reception (and it's not compulsory), it is traditional for the bride and groom to start the first dance on their own. Then, after a while, the bride's father asks to dance with his daughter and the groom then takes the bride's mother to dance. The best man asks the chief bridesmaid to dance and everyone else joins in. And then it's party, party, party until the bride and groom leave.

🔔 **Money, money, money**

In many parts of the world it is traditional for guests to pin banknotes to the brides dress during the dancing to help pay for the honeymoon ...Why don't we do that?

Time to go

When there was a wedding breakfast and that was it, the bride and groom used to go and change, make their farewells, throw the bouquet and drive off on their honeymoon. In some cases that still happens and it's all very straightforward.

The problem is, when you're having a great time at the reception, unless you have a plane to catch, it's easy to get carried away and carry on talking and drinking for hours. Ideally, set a time in advance that you're going to 'leave' (even if you're not actually going away that night) and stick to it. Theoretically, no one else can leave until the bride and groom go. So if you aren't going off on honeymoon that day and are planning to spend all evening partying with all your friends, then stay at the reception venue for the night, have a token 'going away' ceremony, with the throwing of the bouquet (or garter if you want to keep your bouquet) to symbolise the end of the official reception. That way, any of the 'olds' who aren't staying on for the evening can leave without missing anything.

🔔 Throwing the bouquet

In ancient times, the whole village celebrated a marriage. As procreation was the most important thing, after a drunken wedding feast, the bride and groom were 'bedded', with everyone watching them until they were undressed. To try to distract them, the bride would throw one of her stockings over her shoulder. The girl who caught it was supposed to be the next to marry. At the same time, the groom would peel off her garter and throw it over his shoulder for an unmarried male to catch. The lucky man would be the next to marry too. Nowadays we don't usually go into the bridal bedroom with the happy couple so before they depart for their wedding night the bride throws her bouquet over her shoulder for one of the unmarried girls to catch.

Decorating the couple's car

The groom will usually try to hide the car so it doesn't get decorated with nasty things. However, most best men, brothers and other friends usually manage to find it. Favourite decorations are ribbons, balloons, foam to write 'Just married' – or worse – and draw hearts, 'L' plates, old boots and tin cans to tie on the rear bumper. Some more devious 'mates' will even put kippers on the radiator, bangers in the exhaust and confetti all over the seats.

🔔 **Decorating the car**

- The decorating of the car goes back to 'bedding the bride and groom'. Bridesmaids would adorn the bed with ribbons and flowers and this has transferred to decorating the car today.
- Tying shoes or boots on the back of the car dates from Tudor times when shoes were thrown at the couple as they left in their carriage for good luck. It was especially lucky if they or the vehicle were hit.
- Shoes are also a symbol of possession and authority. In Ancient Egypt a pair of the bride's shoes were given to the groom by her father to symbolise the transfer of authority over her from him to the groom and to seal the contract.

The end of a perfect day

When the newlyweds have left, the celebrations may continue without them if this has been arranged beforehand. At the end of the party, the best man, chief bridesmaid and bride's parents (groom's parents too, if they wish) should say goodbye to all the guests. If the parents have already left – which they may do if there has been an evening reception for the younger element – then it's down to the best man, chief bridesmaid and the ushers.

The best man, assisted by the ushers, should remember to collect any of the groom's clothes and belongings and help check nothing has been left behind by any of the guests.

He should also make sure that any cards and telemessages that were read out at the reception are kept for the bride's parents.

The chief bridesmaid, together with the bride's mother if she is still present, should pack up the bride's outfit. She also helps check that nothing has been left behind by any guests.

All the remaining members of the wedding party should help to pack up the presents, if on display, and collect any that were brought on the day. The bride may also have asked that someone gather together small items such as personalised decorations, favours, the book of guest signatures and any disposable cameras, place cards, etc. that have been left on the tables, to put into a box of mementoes.

Chapter 9

The Honeymoon and Beyond

If you intend to go away, the world really is your oyster. But you'll need to book well in advance if you want your first choice.

Most couples like to have a honeymoon – even if it's only a night or two away from home. It doesn't have to be straight after the wedding, but most people prefer it as it they need the rest after all the stress and hype of the wedding! It's also fun to be husband and wife for the first time, and everyone loves honeymoon couples so you can get pretty good treatment if you're prepared to flaunt your new status!

✂£ **Honeymoon on the cheap**

- Book a last-minute deal from www.lastminute.com, www.expedia.com or through your local travel agent.
- Choose a wedding and honeymoon combined deal: it could be cheaper than booking the two separately – either at a home venue or abroad.
- Just go home and enjoy a few days getting used to being Mr and Mrs!

Many tour operators offer special extras including free Champagne, room upgrades, chocolates and flowers for newlyweds, so make sure you tell everyone it's your honeymoon and make the most of it (it won't last long!).

Choose a venue you'd *both* like – and if that means compromising, then you may as well get used to this early on – it's the way forward to a great marriage! It doesn't have to cost a fortune: just a weekend break at a country inn could be so romantic, especially if it's the middle of winter... roaring log fires, four-poster bed, full English breakfast and brisk walks on the hills ... Alternatively, there are loads of inexpensive holidays abroad – look for special offers such as two weeks for the price of one, or one or two free nights' accommodation if you stay for just a few days.

The practicalities are:

- Book early to avoid disappointment, unless you decide to go for a cheap late deal.
- Make sure you have all the relevant documents, such as passports.
- Make sure you have any jabs etc. for more exotic climes well in advance of the wedding (in case of side effects).
- Get your bags packed (and locked!) early and have them stowed in your car ready for your grand exit from the reception.

🔔 Honeymoon secrets

- It is traditional to keep the honeymoon a secret so the couple won't be interrupted on their wedding night.
- The term 'honeymoon' comes from Anglo-Saxon times when a man kidnapped his chosen woman (with the help of his best friend). He would then take her to a secret hiding place to be married and keep her there for a cycle of the moon, after which time her ownership passed to him instead of her father. During this period they drank mead, made from honey.
- In Ireland a laying hen was tied to the bed on the first honeymoon night in the hope that some of its fertility would be passed on to the couple. Eating a double-yolked egg was also thought to bring fertility.
- In Switzerland a pine tree is planted in the couple's garden to symbolise fertility.

The honeymoon's over

The start of a new life! You're back home and there is so much to do – all the presents to open, cake to send to guests who couldn't come (if the bride's mother hasn't done this), legalities to sort out, thank-you letters to write and then at last, you may find time to settle down to being an 'old married couple'.

🔔 New home

When you get to your new home, the groom should carry his new bride over the threshold. There are several superstitions surrounding this idea.

- Evil spells are hidden in the threshold so the groom has to lift his new wife over them so she can begin her new life over spells, not under them!
- It is unlucky for her to step into her new home with her left foot first. One way to avoid this is to be carried.
- It is considered bad luck if the bride trips and falls on her way into the new home, so by carrying her over the threshold that is avoided.
- It is also thought to be from the old Anglo-Saxon custom of the groom stealing his bride and carrying her off.

Thank-you letters

You will have had great fun opening all your presents, and with any luck you remembered at the time to list who gave you what. Now comes the more laborious task of writing to thank everyone. It usually works best if the groom writes to all his friends and family and the bride to hers (on behalf of them both, of course!). Make sure you say what the present was and make the letter personal by including something specific about the gift or the wedding and a bit about the honeymoon if you've had one. It doesn't have to be an epistle, but two lines really aren't enough so do make an effort!

Changing your name

Many women keep their maiden name for professional purposes. In the case of doctors, they are, by convention, always known by the name they held when they qualified. However, if you do change your name when you marry, you will have to notify the following:

- Bank
- Building societies
- Credit card companies
- Dentist
- Doctor
- DVLA (driving licence and car registration certificate)
- Department of Social Security
- Employer
- Inland Revenue
- Insurance companies
- Landlord or mortgage provider
- Lawyer, re making a new will
- Pension provider
- Savings accounts provider
- Stocks and shareholdings broker

> ♤ **Same-letter surnames**
> It used to be thought bad luck for a woman to marry a man with a surname beginning with the same letter:
>
> *To change the name and not the letter*
> *Is to change for the worse and not the better!*
>
> Quite why this should be unlucky, I couldn't find out.

Anniversaries

Technically, anniversaries aren't part of the wedding etiquette but I remember that in the early years of marriage, in particular, you want to celebrate them eagerly. It makes each one that more special if you adhere to the tradition of giving each other a gift in the certain material attached to each one. The big ones everyone knows – silver (25 years), ruby (40 years), gold (50 years) and diamond (60 years) – but some of the others are a little less well known.

Anniversary	Associated material
First	Cotton
Second	Paper
Third	Leather
Fourth	Flowers or silk
Fifth	Wood
Sixth	Sugar
Seventh	Copper

Eighth	Bronze
Ninth	Pottery
Tenth	Tin
Eleventh	Steel
Twelfth	Linen
Thirteenth	Lace
Fourteenth	Ivory
Fifteenth	Crystal
Twentieth	China
Twenty-fifth	Silver
Thirtieth	Pearl
Thirty-fifth	Coral
Fortieth	Ruby
Forty-fifth	Sapphire
Fiftieth	Gold
Fifty-fifth	Emerald
Sixtieth	Diamond
Seventieth	Platinum

If you are going to try to give presents appropriate for each year, it's worth using a little imagination. So for example, for your fifth anniversary, you could plant a tree together and for your thirty-fifth, how about a wonderful holiday of a lifetime on a Caribbean island ... If that's too difficult, you can always buy something in an appropriate colour or texture – but whatever you do, don't forget!

Useful Addresses

This chapter contains the contact details for many of the organisations mentioned in this book, plus a few extras. Note that they are arranged in alphabetical order in each section.

Documentation
Family Record Centre
1 Myddleton Street
Islington
London
EC1R 1UW
Tel: 0870 243 7788
E-mail via website:
www.familyrecords.gov.uk

Religious organisations
Baptist Union of Great Britain
Baptist House
PO Box 44
129 Broadway
Didcot
Oxfordshire OX11 8RT
Tel: 01235 517700
E-mail via website:
www.baptist.org.uk

British Humanist Association
47 Theobolds Road
London WC1X 8SP
Tel: 020 7430 0908

Church of Scotland
121 George Street
Edinburgh EH2 4YN
Tel: 0131 225 5722
E-mail via website:
www.churchofscotland.org.uk

General Synod of the Church of England
Enquiry Centre
Church House
Great Smith Street
London SW1P 3NZ
Tel: 020 7898 1000

Jewish Marriage Council
23 Ravenshurst Avenue
London NW4 2EE
Tel: 020 8203 6311
E-mail via website:
www.jmc-uk.org

Marriage Care
1 Blythe Mews
Blythe Road
London W14 0NW
Tel: 020 7371 1341
E-mail via website:
www.marriagecare.org.uk

Methodist Church Co-ordinating
Secretaries Office
Methodist Church House
25 Marylebone Road
London NW1 5JR
Tel: 020 7486 5502
E-mail via website:
www.methodist.org.uk

Religious Society of Friends
(Quakers)
Friends House
173–177 Euston Road

London NW1 2BJ
Tel: 020 7663 1001
E-mail via the website:
www.quaker.org.uk

Registrar of the Court of
Faculties
1 The Sanctuary
Westminster
London SW1P 3JT
Tel: 0207 222 5381

Representative Body of the
Church of Ireland
Church of Ireland House
Church Avenue
Rathmines
Dublin 6
Tel: 00353 1497 8422

United Reformed Church
Church House
86 Tavistock Place
London WC1H 9RT
Tel: 020 7916 2020
E-mail via website:
www.urc.org.uk

Civil organisations
Foreign and Commonwealth
Office
Consular Division
1 Palace Street
London SW1E 5HE
Tel: 020 7238 4567 (open
9.30 am to 12.30 pm only)

General Register Office for
England and Wales
Smedley Hydro
Trafalgar Road
Southport
PR8 2HH
Tel: 0870 243 7788 (Mon-Fri
8 am to 8 pm, Sat 9 am to 4 pm)
E-mail via the website:
www.statistics.gov.uk/registration

General Register Office for the
Irish Republic
Joyce House
8–11 Lombard Street East
Dublin 2
Eire
Tel: 003531 635 4000

General Register Office for the
Isle of Man
The Civil Registry
Deemster's Walk
Bucks Road
Douglas
Isle of Man IM1 3AR
Tel: 01624 687039
General Register Office for
Northern Ireland
Oxford House
49–55 Chichester Street
Belfast BT1 4HF
Tel: 02890 252000
E-mail via the website:
www.groni.gov.uk

General Register Office for
Scotland
New Register House
Edinburgh EH1 3YT
Tel: 0131 314 4447
E-mail via the website:
www.gro-scotland.gov.uk

Registrar General for Guernsey
The Greffe
Royal Court House
St Peter Port
Guernsey GY1 2PB
Tel: 01481 725 277

Superintendent Registrar for
Jersey
10 Royal Square
St Helier
Jersey JE2 4WA
Tel: 01534 502335

Wedding websites
Browse the following websites
for loads of information and
ideas:
www.confetti.co.uk
www.hitched.co.uk
www.weddingchannel.com
www.weddings-and-brides.co.uk
www.weddingguide.co.uk
www.weddingbells.com
www.webwedding.co.uk

Other useful addresses
British Institute of Professional
Photographers (BIPP)
Fox Talbot House
Ware
Herts SG12 9HN
Tel: 01920 464011
Website: www.bipp.com

The Church House Bookshop
31 Great Smith Street
London SW1P 3BN
Tel: 020 7898 1300

ONS
Local Services
PO Box 56
Southport
PR8 2GL
Tel: 0151 471 4817
E-mail: localservices@ons.gov.uk

Weddings and Honeymoons
Abroad
L & M Business Park
Norman Road
Altrincham
Cheshire WA14 4ES
Tel: 0161 942 9911
Website: www.weddings-abroad.com

The Foulsham Wedding Collection

Chapman, Carole, *Complete Wedding Organiser and Record* (0-572-02338-3)

Chapman, Carole, *Your Wedding Planner* (0-572-02415-0)

Derraugh, Pat and Bill, *Wedding Etiquette* (0-572-02409-6)

Eames, Jacqueline, *Best Best Man* (0-572-02339-1)

Hobson, Christopher, *Best Man's Organiser* (0-572-02303-0)

Hobson, Wendy, *Best Man's Last-minute Organiser: Essentials* (0-572-02975-6)

Hobson, Wendy, and Chapman, Carole, *Wedding Duties for Men: Essentials* (0-572-02761-3)

Hobson, Wendy, with Onslow, Paula, *Your Wedding File and Gift List* (0-572-02953-5)

Janes, Matthew, *Living Together as Partners* (0-572-02764-8)

Onslow, Paula, *Plan Your Wedding Gift List: Essentials* (0-572-02962-4)

Smith, Helen, *Your Brilliant Wedding Speech: Essentials* (0-572-02762-1)

Statham, Amanda, *Getting Married Abroad* (0-572-02920-9)

Statham, Amanda, *Modern Bride: Essentials* (0-572-02870-9)

Wynburne, Revd John, and Gibbs, Alison, *Wedding Readings and Musical Ideas* (0-572-02861-X)

Index